GREAT EXPECTATIONS

THE ELT GRAPHIC NOVEL
Charles Dickens

Script by Jen Green
Adapted for ELT by Brigit Viney

HEINLE
CENGAGE Learning™

Australia • Brazil • Japan • Korea • Mexico • Singapore • Spain • United Kingdom • United States

HEINLE
CENGAGE Learning

Great Expectations: The Graphic ELT Novel
Charles Dickens
Script by Jen Green
Adapted for ELT by Brigit Viney

Publisher: Jason Mann

Editor in Chief: Clive Bryant

Managing and Development Editor:
   Jennifer Nunan

Assistant Editors: Victoria Chappell and
   Heidi North

Contributing Writer: Amanda Cole

Head of Marketing: Ruth McAleavey

Content Project Editor: Natalie Griffith

Manufacturing Manager: Helen Mason

Cover / Text Designer: Jo Wheeler

Compositor: Jo Wheeler, Jenny
   Placentino and Macmillan
   Publishing Solutions

Character Designs & Original Artwork:
   John Stokes

Colouring: Digikore Studios Ltd.

Colour Finishing: Jason Cardy

Lettering: Jim Campbell

Audio: EFS Television Production Ltd.

ISBN: 978-1-4240-2879-5

Heinle, Cengage Learning EMEA
Cheriton House
North Way
Andover
Hampshire
SP10 5BE
United Kingdom

Cengage Learning is a leading provider of customized learning solutions with office locations around the globe, including Singapore, the United Kingdom, Australia, Mexico, Brazil and Japan. Locate our local office at: **international.cengage.com/region**

Cengage Learning products are represented in Canada by Nelson Education, Ltd.

Visit Heinle online at **elt.heinle.com**
Visit our corporate website at **cengage.com**

Published in association with Classical Comics Ltd.

Printed in Mexico
3 4 5 6 7 8 9 10 – 13 12 11

Contents

Characters

Young Pip
A boy who lives with his sister and her husband because his parents are dead

Adult Pip

Miss Havisham
A rich old lady

Abel Magwitch
A prisoner who has escaped

Older Magwitch

Joe Gargery
The husband of Pip's sister

Mrs Joe Gargery
Pip's sister, and wife of Joe Gargery

Young Estella
*Miss Havisham's **adopted** daughter*

Adult Estella

Young Biddy
Granddaughter of Mr. Wopsle's great–aunt

Adult Biddy

Herbert Pocket
Son of Mr Matthew Pocket

Characters

Mr Matthew Pocket
A relation of Miss Havisham

Sarah Pocket
A relation of Miss Havisham

Clara Barley
Young woman that Herbert Pocket wants to marry

Bentley Drummle
Student who is taught by Mr Matthew Pocket

Startop
Student who is taught by Mr Matthew Pocket

Mr Jaggers
A lawyer from London

John Wemmick
Clerk who works for Mr Jaggers

Wemmick's father

Molly
Mr Jaggers's housekeeper

Dolge Orlick
Blacksmith who works for Joe Gargery

Compeyson
Prisoner

Mr Pumblechook
Joe Gargery's uncle

Introduction

The year is 1812.

In the south-east corner of England, there are some large **marshes**. They are about thirty miles from the City of London. They lie between the River Thames and the River Medway, and they go down to the sea. They are cold, wet and **misty**. Not many people live near them — there are only a few small villages.

Some large ships lie in the sea near the marshes. Hundreds of **prisoners** are held in them. Soon these men will be taken to Australia. They will have to stay away from Britain for the rest of their lives. This is their punishment. From the ships they can see the lonely, silent marshes — just the sort of place where someone could hide ...

WHO DO YOU LIVE WITH?

MY SISTER, SIR – MRS JOE GARGERY – WIFE OF JOE GARGERY, THE **BLACKSMITH**, SIR.

BLACKSMITH? THEN GET ME A **FILE**, AND FOOD.

BRING THEM TO ME AT THAT OLD **BATTERY** EARLY TOMORROW MORNING,

OR I'LL TEAR YOUR HEART OUT!

I'M NOT ALONE.

THERE'S A YOUNG MAN WITH ME, WHO HAS A SECRET WAY OF GETTING TO BOYS AND TEARING OUT THEIR HEARTS.

SO – WHAT DO YOU THINK?

I'LL GET YOU THE FILE AND FOOD.

HE WALKED AWAY THEN, AND CLIMBED OVER THE CHURCH WALL. I RAN HOME.

VOLUME I
CHAPTER II

MY SISTER, MRS JOE GARGERY, WAS MUCH OLDER THAN I.

JOE GARGERY, THE **BLACKSMITH**, WAS A GENTLE, KIND, DEAR MAN. HIS **FORGE** WAS NEXT TO OUR HOUSE.

JOE WAS SITTING ALONE IN THE KITCHEN.

MRS JOE'S BEEN LOOKING FOR YOU, PIP, AND SHE'S GOT TICKLER WITH HER.

OH! SHE'S COMING! GET BEHIND THE DOOR!

TICKLER WAS A STICK THAT SHE USED TO HIT ME WITH.

WHERE HAVE YOU BEEN, YOU YOUNG MONKEY?

ONLY TO THE **CHURCHYARD**.

CHURCHYARD! YOU'RE LUCKY YOU AREN'T LYING THERE!

THWACK THWACK

WHO **BROUGHT** YOU **UP**?

YOU DID.

I DID! AND I'D NEVER DO IT AGAIN! BEING YOUR MOTHER HAS BEEN HARD WORK.

YOU'LL DRIVE *ME* TO THE CHURCHYARD ONE OF THESE DAYS.

BOOOOOOMMM!!

WAS THAT A **GUN**, JOE?

ANOTHER **PRISONER'S** ESCAPED. ONE ESCAPED LAST NIGHT AND THEY **FIRED** THE GUN AS A WARNING THEN, AND NOW THERE'S ANOTHER WARNING!

11

**VOLUME I
CHAPTER III**

I KNEW MY WAY TO THE **BATTERY** BECAUSE I'D BEEN THERE WITH JOE.

WHEN I WAS ALMOST THERE, I FOUND A MAN. HE WAS ASLEEP. I TOUCHED HIM ON THE SHOULDER.

IT WAS NOT THE SAME MAN!

I THOUGHT IT WAS THE OTHER MAN, AND MY HEART BEAT VERY FAST.

HE RAN OFF INTO THE FOG. I WENT ON TO THE BATTERY ...

... AND THERE WAS THE RIGHT MAN. HE WAS VERY COLD AND HUNGRY.

I'M AFRAID YOU WON'T LEAVE ANY FOR HIM.

THE YOUNG MAN WHO'S HIDING WITH YOU.

WHO'S 'HIM'?

HIM? HE DOESN'T WANT ANY FOOD.

HE LOOKED AS IF HE DID. I JUST SAW HIM OVER THERE.

SHOW ME WHERE HE WENT! I MUST GET THIS LEG-IRON OFF! GIVE ME THE FILE, BOY!

I SHOWED HIM THE DIRECTION IN WHICH THE MAN HAD GONE.

HE LOOKED UP FOR A MOMENT. THEN HE BEGAN USING THE FILE ON HIS LEG-IRON. HE WORKED LIKE A MADMAN.

I WAS VERY AFRAID AGAIN, SO I RAN HOME.

VOLUME I
CHAPTER IV

I EXPECTED TO FIND A POLICEMAN IN THE KITCHEN, BUT THERE WASN'T ONE. IN FACT, NO ONE HAD NOTICED THE ROBBERY.

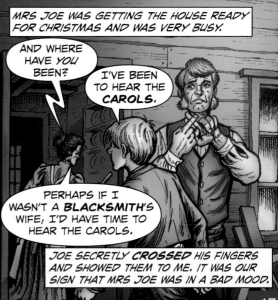

MRS JOE WAS GETTING THE HOUSE READY FOR CHRISTMAS AND WAS VERY BUSY.

AND WHERE HAVE YOU BEEN?

I'VE BEEN TO HEAR THE CAROLS.

PERHAPS IF I WASN'T A BLACKSMITH'S WIFE, I'D HAVE TIME TO HEAR THE CAROLS.

JOE SECRETLY CROSSED HIS FINGERS AND SHOWED THEM TO ME. IT WAS OUR SIGN THAT MRS JOE WAS IN A BAD MOOD.

WHERE'S THE PIE GONE?

I COULDN'T BEAR ANY MORE, SO I RAN FROM THE TABLE.

HERE YOU ARE!

VOLUME I CHAPTER V

EXCUSE ME, LADIES AND GENTLEMEN. I'M SEARCHING FOR SOME **PRISONERS** WHO'VE ESCAPED. I WANT THE **BLACKSMITH.**

AND WHAT DO YOU WANT WITH HIM?

JUST TO DO A LITTLE JOB FOR THE KING. BLACKSMITH, WE'VE HAD AN ACCIDENT WITH THESE, AND WE NEED THEM NOW. WILL YOU LOOK AT THEM?

WHEN I REALISED THAT THE **HANDCUFFS** WERE NOT FOR ME, I RELAXED. JOE BEGAN TO FIX THE HANDCUFFS AND WE ALL WATCHED.

AT LAST JOE FINISHED. THEN HE, I AND MR WOPSLE WENT OUT WITH THE SOLDIERS ON THEIR HUNT.

I hope we don't find them, Joe.

Yes, I hope they've got away.

I WAS AFRAID OF MEETING MY PRISONER. HE MIGHT THINK I HAD BROUGHT THE SOLDIERS THERE.

WE WERE MOVING IN THE DIRECTION OF THE **BATTERY**, WHEN WE HEARD SHOUTS IN THE DISTANCE.

MURDER!

QUICKLY!

GUARDS! THIS WAY!

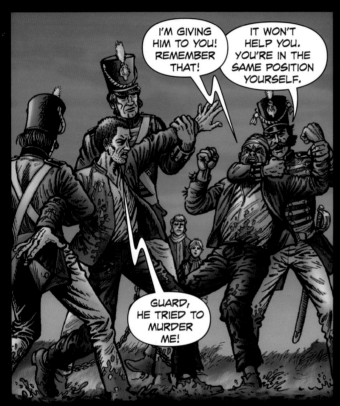

AFTER AN HOUR OF TRAVELLING, WE REACHED A WOODEN *HUT*.

I WISH TO TELL YOU SOMETHING ABOUT THIS ESCAPE.

I STOLE SOME FOOD FROM THE **BLACKSMITH'S** IN THE VILLAGE.

MY WIFE SAW SOME WAS MISSING.

SO YOU'RE THE BLACKSMITH, ARE YOU? I'M SORRY I'VE EATEN YOUR PIE.

YOU'RE WELCOME TO IT. WE WOULDN'T LIKE YOU TO DIE OF HUNGER, WOULD WE, PIP?

VOLUME I
CHAPTER VI

BY THE LIGHT OF THE *TORCHES* WE SAW THE BLACK HULK. THE *PRISONER* WAS TAKEN UP ITS SIDE AND THEN HE DISAPPEARED INTO IT. THE TORCHES WERE THROWN INTO THE WATER.

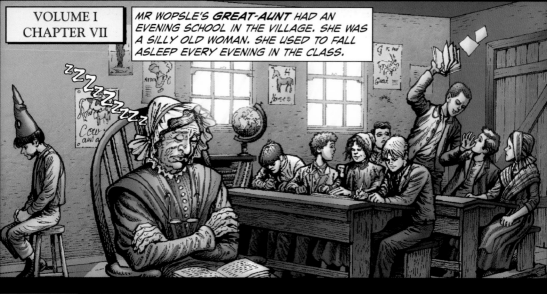

MR WOPSLE'S **GREAT-AUNT** HAD AN EVENING SCHOOL IN THE VILLAGE. SHE WAS A SILLY OLD WOMAN. SHE USED TO FALL ASLEEP EVERY EVENING IN THE CLASS.

IT WAS BIDDY WHO TAUGHT ME MY LETTERS. SHE WAS THE GRANDDAUGHTER OF MR WOPSLE'S GREAT-AUNT. HER PARENTS WERE DEAD, LIKE MINE.

ONE NIGHT I SAT AT HOME AND TRIED TO WRITE A LETTER TO JOE.

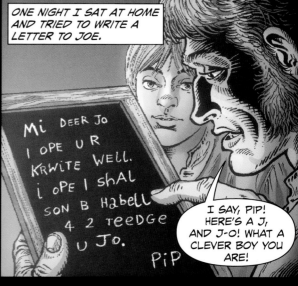

Mi DEER Jo
I OPE U R
KRWITE WELL.
i OPE I ShAL
SON B HabELL
4 2 TEEDGE
U Jo.
PiP

I SAY, PIP! HERE'S A J, AND J-O! WHAT A CLEVER BOY YOU ARE!

I OFFERED TO TEACH HIM MORE LETTERS.

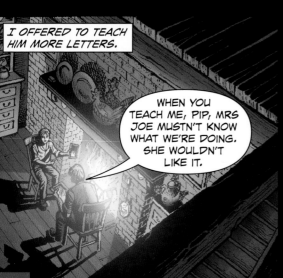

WHEN YOU TEACH ME, PIP, MRS JOE MUSTN'T KNOW WHAT WE'RE DOING. SHE WOULDN'T LIKE IT.

I KNOW THAT YOUR SISTER IS HARD ON US. WHY DON'T I DEFEND US? WELL, SHE'S VERY CLEVER, AND I'M NOT. BUT TICKLER IS HARD FOR YOU, OLD **CHAP**, I KNOW. IT'S NEARLY EIGHT O'CLOCK, AND SHE'S STILL NOT HOME.

HERE'S THE HORSE!

IF THE BOY ISN'T **GRATEFUL** TONIGHT, HE NEVER WILL BE! I HOPE SHE WON'T **SPOIL** HIM.

WHO?

SHE WON'T DO THAT.

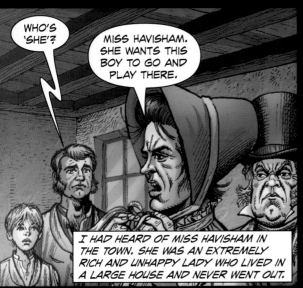

WHO'S 'SHE'?

MISS HAVISHAM. SHE WANTS THIS BOY TO GO AND PLAY THERE.

I HAD HEARD OF MISS HAVISHAM IN THE TOWN. SHE WAS AN EXTREMELY RICH AND UNHAPPY LADY WHO LIVED IN A LARGE HOUSE AND NEVER WENT OUT.

I WONDER HOW SHE KNOWS PIP!

WHO SAID SHE KNEW HIM? SHE KNOWS **UNCLE** PUMBLECHOOK. SHE ASKED HIM IF HE KNEW A BOY WHO COULD PLAY THERE.

HEAVENS! I'M STANDING HERE WHILE MR PUMBLECHOOK'S WAITING, AND THE BOY'S COVERED IN DIRT!

SPLOOSH

BOY, BE GRATEFUL TO ALL YOUR FRIENDS, BUT ESPECIALLY TO THOSE THAT **BROUGHT** YOU **UP!**

GOODBYE, PIP, OLD **CHAP!**

THE NEXT MORNING, MR PUMBLECHOOK AND I HAD BREAKFAST. AT TEN O'CLOCK WE WENT TO SATIS HOUSE, THE HOME OF MISS HAVISHAM. WHEN WE ARRIVED, WE RANG THE **BELL** AND WAITED AT THE GATE.

THIS IS PIP.

THIS IS PIP, IS IT? COME IN, PIP.

HURRY UP, BOY.

WE WENT INTO THE HOUSE THROUGH A SIDE DOOR. ALL THE **PASSAGES** WERE DARK. ONLY THE CANDLE SHOWED US THE WAY UP THE STAIRS. AT LAST WE CAME TO THE DOOR OF A ROOM.

AFTER YOU, MISS.

DON'T BE **STUPID**, BOY. I'M NOT GOING IN.

SHE WALKED AWAY AND TOOK THE CANDLE WITH HER. I FELT AFRAID.

KNOCK

KNOCK

COME IN!

DO YOU KNOW WHAT I'M TOUCHING HERE?

YES, MA'AM. YOUR HEART.

BROKEN! I WANT TO WATCH YOU WHILE YOU PLAY. PLAY!

DO YOU REFUSE TO PLAY?

NO, MA'AM. I WOULD PLAY IF I COULD, BUT IT'S SO NEW HERE, AND SO STRANGE AND FINE AND SAD ...

So new to him, so old to me. So strange to him, so familiar to me. So sad to us both!

CALL ESTELLA. YOU CAN DO THAT AT THE DOOR.

ESTELLA !!!

ESTELLA'S LIGHT CAME ALONG THE DARK PASSAGE LIKE A STAR. MISS HAVISHAM CALLED HER TO HER AND HELD A JEWEL AGAINST HER PRETTY BROWN HAIR.

IT WILL BE YOURS ONE DAY, MY DEAR. YOU'LL USE IT WELL.

NOW PLAY CARDS WITH THIS BOY.

WITH HIM? HE'S A COMMON WORKING BOY! WHAT CAN YOU PLAY, BOY?

ONLY ONE GAME, MISS.

PLAY THAT. BEAT HIM, ESTELLA.

SO WE PLAYED CARDS.

MISS HAVISHAM SAT AS STILL AS A DEAD WOMAN WHILE WE PLAYED. ESTELLA COMPLAINED BEFORE WE HAD FINISHED THE FIRST GAME.

WHAT ROUGH HANDS HE HAS! AND WHAT THICK BOOTS!

I HAD NEVER BEEN ASHAMED OF MY HANDS BEFORE, BUT I BEGAN TO FEEL ASHAMED THEN.

23

ESTELLA WON THE GAME, AND I DEALT THE CARDS FOR THE NEXT GAME BUT I DEALT THEM WRONGLY. SHE SAID I WAS A **STUPID** WORKING BOY.

YOU DON'T SAY ANYTHING ABOUT HER, AND SHE IS SO UNKIND TO YOU.

WHAT DO YOU THINK OF HER? TELL ME IN MY EAR.

She is very proud, very pretty and very **rude**.

ANYTHING ELSE?

I'D LIKE TO GO HOME.

YOU CAN GO SOON. FINISH THE GAME.

WE FINISHED THE GAME.

COME AGAIN IN SIX DAYS.

ESTELLA, TAKE HIM DOWN. GIVE HIM SOMETHING TO EAT AND LET HIM LOOK AROUND.

I FOLLOWED THE CANDLE BACK DOWN THE STAIRS. WHEN ESTELLA OPENED THE SIDE DOOR, I WAS SHOCKED BY THE SUDDEN **DAYLIGHT**.

WAIT HERE, BOY.

SHE DISAPPEARED AND CLOSED THE DOOR.

ALONE, I LOOKED AT MY ROUGH HANDS AND THICK BOOTS. THEY HAD NEVER TROUBLED ME BEFORE, BUT THEY TROUBLED ME NOW.

SHE CAME BACK WITH SOME BREAD, MEAT AND **BEER**. SHE GAVE IT TO ME BUT DIDN'T LOOK AT ME. I WAS LIKE A BAD DOG.

I WAS VERY HURT. I WANTED TO CRY, BUT I DIDN'T.

WHEN SHE HAD GONE, I HID MY FACE AND CRIED.

WHEN I HAD STOPPED CRYING, I LOOKED AROUND.

I WENT INTO THE GARDEN AND THEN INTO THE LARGE **BREWERY** AT THE SIDE OF THE HOUSE. IT WAS EMPTY BECAUSE NO ONE USED IT ANY MORE.

I SAW A FIGURE. IT WAS HANGING BY THE NECK. IT WAS IN YELLOW-WHITE AND IT HAD MISS HAVISHAM'S FACE.

I WAS TERRIFIED. WHEN I RAN TOWARDS IT, IT HAD GONE. THIS TERRIFIED ME EVEN MORE.

GASP!

WHEN I WAS BACK IN THE **DAYLIGHT**, I FELT BETTER. ESTELLA CAME WITH THE KEYS TO LET ME OUT.

WHY DON'T YOU CRY?

BECAUSE I DON'T WANT TO.

YES, YOU DO. YOU'VE BEEN CRYING UNTIL YOU'RE HALF-**BLIND**, AND YOU'RE NEARLY CRYING NOW.

HA, HA, HA!

SHE LOCKED THE GATE BEHIND ME AND I STARTED WALKING HOME. I THOUGHT A LOT ABOUT MY ROUGH HANDS AND MY THICK BOOTS. I THOUGHT ABOUT BEING A COMMON WORKING BOY.

WHEN I GOT HOME, MR PUMBLECHOOK WAS THERE.

WELL, BOY, HOW DID IT GO?

QUITE WELL, SIR.

QUITE WELL? THAT'S NO ANSWER!

WHAT WAS MISS HAVISHAM DOING?

SHE WAS SITTING IN A BLACK COACH. AND MISS ESTELLA GAVE HER CAKE AND **WINE** ON A GOLD PLATE. WE ALL HAD CAKE AND WINE ON GOLD PLATES.

THERE WERE FOUR HUGE DOGS AND THEY FOUGHT FOR MEAT OUT OF A SILVER BASKET.

CAN THIS BE POSSIBLE, **UNCLE**?

IT COULD BE A **SEDAN CHAIR**. SHE COULD SPEND HER DAYS IN A SEDAN CHAIR.

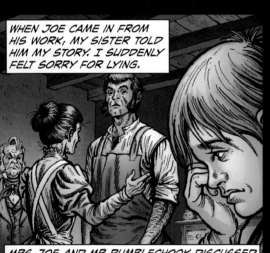

WHEN JOE CAME IN FROM HIS WORK, MY SISTER TOLD HIM MY STORY. I SUDDENLY FELT SORRY FOR LYING.

MRS JOE AND MR PUMBLECHOOK DISCUSSED MISS HAVISHAM. THEY WERE SURE SHE WOULD HELP ME OR GIVE ME SOMETHING.

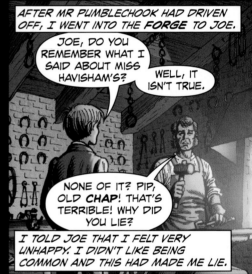

AFTER MR PUMBLECHOOK HAD DRIVEN OFF, I WENT INTO THE **FORGE** TO JOE.

JOE, DO YOU REMEMBER WHAT I SAID ABOUT MISS HAVISHAM'S?

WELL, IT ISN'T TRUE.

NONE OF IT? PIP, OLD **CHAP**! THAT'S TERRIBLE! WHY DID YOU LIE?

I TOLD JOE THAT I FELT VERY UNHAPPY. I DIDN'T LIKE BEING COMMON AND THIS HAD MADE ME LIE.

LIES ARE LIES, PIP. DON'T TELL ANY MORE OF THEM. THEY AREN'T THE WAY TO STOP BEING COMMON. AND YOU AREN'T COMMON IN EVERYTHING. YOU'RE AN UNCOMMON STUDENT.

NO, I'M NOT, JOE. I'M SLOW AND I DON'T KNOW MUCH.

WELL, PIP, YOU MUST BE COMMON BEFORE YOU CAN BE UNCOMMON! EVEN A KING HAS TO LEARN HIS LETTERS!

THERE WAS SOME HOPE IN THIS AND IT ENCOURAGED ME.

A DAY LATER, I THOUGHT OF A WAY NOT TO BE COMMON. I COULD GET BIDDY TO TEACH ME ALL SHE KNEW.

I ASKED HER, AND SHE IMMEDIATELY AGREED.

NO ONE ELSE SAW THE **FILE**.

I KNEW IT WAS THE FILE I HAD GIVEN THE **PRISONER**. I KNEW THAT HE KNEW MY PRISONER.

THE STRANGER TOOK LITTLE NOTICE OF ME. AFTER HALF AN HOUR, JOE GOT UP TO GO.

WAIT A MOMENT, MR GARGERY. I'VE GOT A **SHILLING** FOR THE BOY.

HE PUT IT IN SOME PAPER.

IT'S JUST YOURS!

THANK YOU, SIR.

JOE AND I SAID GOODNIGHT AND WALKED HOME.

MY SISTER WAS NOT IN A BAD MOOD WHEN WE GOT HOME, SO JOE TOLD HER ABOUT THE SHILLING.

HE'S A BAD ONE, THEN! LET ME SEE IT.

WHAT'S THIS? TWO ONE-POUND NOTES?

JOE TOOK THEM BACK TO THE **PUB**, BUT THE MAN HAD GONE. MY SISTER HID THEM IN THE FRONT SITTING-ROOM. THEY REMAINED THERE, A WORRY TO ME, FOR A LONG TIME.

I RETURNED TO MISS HAVISHAM'S, AS SHE HAD ASKED. ESTELLA CAME TO THE GATE AND LED ME INTO A DARK **PASSAGE**.

COME THIS WAY TODAY.

SHE TOOK ME DOWN THE LONG PASSAGE, AND ACROSS A SMALL **COURTYARD**, TO ANOTHER HOUSE. IT HAD PROBABLY BEEN THE HOUSE OF THE **BREWERY** MANAGER. WE ENTERED A DARK ROOM. THREE LADIES AND A **GENTLEMAN** WERE THERE. THEY STOPPED TALKING WHEN WE CAME IN AND LOOKED AT ME.

STAND THERE, BOY, UNTIL YOU'RE WANTED.

THE LADIES AND GENTLEMAN SEEMED AS IF THEY WERE WAITING FOR SOMEONE.

POOR MAN! MATTHEW IS HIS OWN WORST **ENEMY**!

WE SHOULD LOVE OUR NEIGHBOUR, YOU KNOW.

POOR MAN! HE'S SO STRANGE.

DING A LING

NOW, BOY!

AS WE WERE GOING ALONG THE DARK PASSAGE, ESTELLA SUDDENLY STOPPED AND TURNED TO ME.

AM I PRETTY?

YES, I THINK YOU ARE VERY PRETTY.

AM I **RUDE**?

NOT AS MUCH AS YOU WERE LAST TIME.

I WENT INTO THE ROOM SHE POINTED TO. IT WAS LARGE AND DARK. EVERYTHING IN IT WAS COVERED IN **DUST.** THERE WAS A LONG TABLE AND ON IT WERE PREPARATIONS FOR A MEAL FOR MANY PEOPLE. THE PREPARATIONS HAD STOPPED WHEN THE HOUSE AND CLOCKS HAD STOPPED.

THERE WAS SOMETHING LARGE IN THE CENTRE OF THE TABLE. SPIDERS WERE RUNNING IN AND OUT OF IT.

THAT'S MY **WEDDING** CAKE!

COME! WALK WITH ME!

I BEGAN TO WALK WITH HER ROUND AND ROUND THE ROOM.

DEAR MISS HAVISHAM! HOW WELL YOU LOOK!

NO I DON'T, SARAH POCKET! I AM YELLOW SKIN AND BONE.

MISS HAVISHAM KNEW THAT ALL THEIR EXPRESSIONS OF KINDNESS WERE FALSE.

MATTHEW NEVER COMES TO SEE MISS HAVISHAM!

HE WILL COME TO SEE ME WHEN I AM DEAD AND LAID ON THAT TABLE.

HE'LL STAND AT MY HEAD.

AND YOU WILL STAND THERE! AND YOUR HUSBAND THERE! AND SARAH POCKET THERE!

NOW GO!

WE SUPPOSE WE MUST LEAVE THEN.

GOODBYE, MISS HAVISHAM DEAR!

IT'S MY BIRTHDAY TODAY, PIP.

ON THIS DAY, MANY YEARS AGO, ALL THESE THINGS WERE BROUGHT HERE. THEY AND I HAVE GOT OLD TOGETHER.

SHE STOOD AND LOOKED AT THE TABLE. I REMAINED QUIET.

ESTELLA CAME BACK, AND A DAY WAS ARRANGED FOR MY RETURN. I WAS TAKEN TO THE **COURTYARD** AND FED LIKE A DOG AGAIN. THEN I WAS ABLE TO WALK AROUND ON MY OWN AGAIN.

AFTER WALKING ROUND THE GARDEN, I FOUND MYSELF AT THE HOUSE WHERE I HAD WAITED EARLIER. I THOUGHT IT WAS EMPTY, SO I LOOKED IN AT A WINDOW.

TO MY GREAT SURPRISE, A **PALE YOUNG GENTLEMAN** LOOKED BACK AT ME.

HE QUICKLY DISAPPEARED AND THEN REAPPEARED BESIDE ME.

HELLO, YOUNG MAN! WHO LET YOU IN?

MISS ESTELLA.

COME AND FIGHT!

I WAS SO SURPRISED THAT I FOLLOWED HIM.

AARRGH!

DOOFFF!

THWUMMPP!

AT LAST HE FELL AGAINST THE WALL.

YOU'VE WON.

CAN I HELP YOU?

NO THANKS. GOOD AFTERNOON.

I WISHED HERBERT A GOOD AFTERNOON AND WENT BACK TO THE *COURTYARD*. ESTELLA WAS WAITING THERE. SHE LOOKED EXCITED.

COME HERE! YOU MAY KISS ME, IF YOU LIKE.

I KISSED HER *CHEEK*.

I FELT SHE GAVE IT TO THE COMMON WORKING BOY LIKE A PIECE OF MONEY.

I WAS SURE THAT I WOULD GET INTO TROUBLE FOR THE FIGHT. EVERY TIME I LEFT THE HOUSE, I LOOKED OUT OF THE DOOR CAREFULLY FIRST. I WAS AFRAID THE POLICE MIGHT COME FOR ME.

WHEN I HAD TO RETURN TO MISS HAVISHAM'S, I BECAME VERY FRIGHTENED. HOWEVER, I HAD TO GO, SO I DID.

NO ONE SAID ANYTHING ABOUT THE FIGHT! AND THE **PALE** YOUNG **GENTLEMAN** WASN'T THERE.

I PUSHED MISS HAVISHAM IN A WHEELCHAIR ROUND HER OWN ROOM AND ROUND THE OTHER ROOM. THIS BECAME A REGULAR OCCUPATION. SOMETIMES OUR JOURNEYS LASTED AS LONG AS THREE HOURS.

Does she grow prettier and prettier, Pip?

Yes.

I WENT TO MISS HAVISHAM'S EVERY SECOND DAY AT NOON AND PUSHED HER IN HER WHEELCHAIR. I DID THIS FOR ABOUT EIGHT OR TEN MONTHS.

ESTELLA WAS ALWAYS THERE, BUT SHE NEVER LET ME KISS HER AGAIN. SOMETIMES SHE WAS COLD TO ME, SOMETIMES SHE WAS QUITE FRIENDLY, SOMETIMES SHE TOLD ME SHE HATED ME.

Break their hearts, my dear. Break their hearts and have no pity!

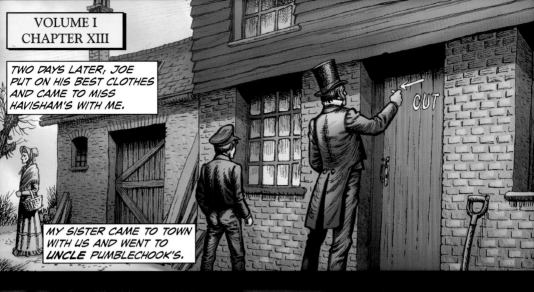

TWO DAYS LATER, JOE PUT ON HIS BEST CLOTHES AND CAME TO MISS HAVISHAM'S WITH ME.

CUT

MY SISTER CAME TO TOWN WITH US AND WENT TO **UNCLE** PUMBLECHOOK'S.

AT MISS HAVISHAM'S HOUSE, ESTELLA OPENED THE GATE AS USUAL. SHE IGNORED US BOTH AS SHE TOOK US UP TO MISS HAVISHAM.

GO IN.

DURING THE INTERVIEW, JOE SPOKE ONLY TO ME, NOT TO MISS HAVISHAM.

I BELIEVE YOU WISH PIP TO BECOME YOUR **APPRENTICE**, MR GARGERY. IS THAT RIGHT?

AS YOU AND I ARE FRIENDS, PIP, WE HAVE **LOOKED FORWARD TO** WORKING TOGETHER. BUT YOU CAN SAY IF YOU DON'T WANT TO WORK WITH ME.

HAVE YOU BROUGHT HIS CONTRACT WITH YOU?

WELL, PIP, YOU KNOW IT'S IN MY HAT.

DON'T YOU EXPECT A PAYMENT FOR THE BOY?

PIP, YOU KNOW THE ANSWER TO THAT IS NO.

PIP HAS EARNED MONEY HERE, AND HERE IT IS. THERE ARE TWENTY-FIVE POUNDS IN THIS BAG. GIVE IT TO YOUR **MASTER**, PIP.

THIS IS VERY KIND, PIP, AND IS **GRATEFULLY** RECEIVED, ALTHOUGH NOT AT ALL EXPECTED.

GOODBYE, PIP! LET THEM OUT, ESTELLA.

SHOULD I COME AGAIN, MISS HAVISHAM?

NO. GARGERY IS YOUR MASTER NOW.

WELL? WHAT HAPPENED?

MISS HAVISHAM SENDS HER BEST WISHES TO MRS J. GARGERY —

THEY'RE NO USE TO ME! WHAT DID SHE GIVE HIM?

NOTHING.

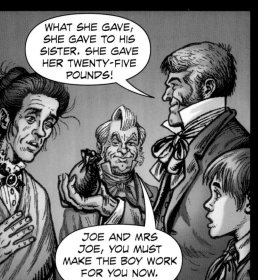

WHAT SHE GAVE, SHE GAVE TO HIS SISTER. SHE GAVE HER TWENTY-FIVE POUNDS!

JOE AND MRS JOE, YOU MUST MAKE THE BOY WORK FOR YOU NOW.

WE IMMEDIATELY WENT TO THE **TOWN HALL**. IN FRONT OF A JUDGE, I WAS MADE JOE'S **APPRENTICE**.

What's he done?

He's young, but he looks bad, doesn't he?

MY SISTER BECAME SO EXCITED THAT WE HAD DINNER AT THE BLUE **BOAR**. IT WAS A VERY SAD DAY FOR ME. I HAD TO STAND ON A CHAIR BESIDE PUMBLECHOOK WHILE HE SPOKE ABOUT ME.

THEY WOULDN'T LET ME GO TO SLEEP. EACH TIME I BEGAN TO FALL ASLEEP, THEY WOKE ME UP. THEY TOLD ME TO ENJOY MYSELF.

WHEN I FINALLY GOT INTO MY LITTLE BEDROOM, I WAS VERY **MISERABLE**. I KNEW THAT I WOULDN'T LIKE JOE'S WORK.

I HAD LIKED IT, BUT I DIDN'T LIKE IT NOW.

IT IS VERY **MISERABLE** TO FEEL ASHAMED OF YOUR HOME. HOME HAD NEVER BEEN VERY PLEASANT, BUT IT HAD HAD JOE, AND I HAD BELIEVED IN IT. NOW I THOUGHT IT WAS POOR AND COMMON.

I USED TO STAND IN THE **CHURCHYARD** ON SUNDAY EVENINGS AND LOOK OUT AT THE **MARSHES**. WHAT DID I WANT? I DIDN'T KNOW. I DIDN'T WANT ESTELLA TO SEE ME AT THE **FORGE** WHEN I WAS VERY DIRTY.

VOLUME I CHAPTER XV

I WAS GETTING TOO BIG FOR MR WOPSLE'S **GREAT-AUNT'S** ROOM, SO MY EDUCATION THERE ENDED. HOWEVER, BIDDY HAD TAUGHT ME EVERYTHING SHE KNEW. WHATEVER I LEARNT FROM HER, I TRIED TO TEACH TO JOE.

I ONLY DID THIS TO MAKE JOE LESS COMMON. I DID NOT THINK HE WAS GOOD ENOUGH FOR ME.

JOE, DON'T YOU THINK I OUGHT TO VISIT MISS HAVISHAM?

WELL, PIP, WHAT FOR?

I'M IN MY FIRST YEAR OF WORK, AND I'VE NEVER THANKED HER.

WOULD YOU GIVE ME A HALF-DAY'S HOLIDAY TOMORROW? I COULD GO TO TOWN AND VISIT MISS EST-HAVISHAM.

HER NAME ISN'T ESTAVISHAM, PIP.

I KNOW, JOE. IT WAS A MISTAKE. WHAT DO YOU THINK? CAN I GO?

JOE AGREED, BUT SAID THAT IF THEY DIDN'T RECEIVE ME POLITELY, I COULD NOT GO AGAIN. I AGREED TO THIS CONDITION.

MY SISTER **FAINTED**. JOE CARRIED HER INTO THE HOUSE, AND I DRESSED TO GO TO MISS HAVISHAM'S.

MISS SARAH POCKET LET ME IN. EVERYTHING WAS UNCHANGED, AND MISS HAVISHAM WAS ALONE. ESTELLA WASN'T THERE.

ARE YOU LOOKING FOR ESTELLA?

I H-H-HOPE THAT SHE IS W-W-WELL.

SHE'S ABROAD. SHE'S LEARNING TO BE A LADY, FAR AWAY. DO YOU FEEL THAT YOU HAVE LOST HER?

SHE DIDN'T WAIT FOR MY ANSWER, AND TOLD ME TO LEAVE.

WHEN I WAS OUTSIDE THE GATE, I FELT MORE UNHAPPY WITH MY HOME AND WORK THAN BEFORE.

I WAS WALKING ALONG THE HIGH STREET WHEN I MET MR WOPSLE. HE MADE ME GO WITH HIM TO *UNCLE PUMBLECHOOK'S*. IT WAS VERY DARK WHEN WE BEGAN TO WALK HOME. ON THE WAY WE MET ORLICK.

SOME **PRISONERS** HAVE ESCAPED FROM THE HULKS AGAIN.

WHEN WE REACHED THE *PUB* IN THE VILLAGE, WE HEARD A LOT OF NOISE FROM INSIDE. MR WOPSLE WENT IN TO ASK WHAT WAS THE MATTER. HE RAN OUT IN A GREAT HURRY.

SOMETHING'S HAPPENED AT YOUR PLACE, PIP!

SOMEONE'S HURT! RUN!

OUR KITCHEN WAS FULL OF PEOPLE AND MY SISTER WAS LYING ON THE FLOOR.

SOMEONE HAD HIT HER VERY HARD ON THE BACK OF THE HEAD.

NEXT TO HER LAY A *LEG-IRON*.

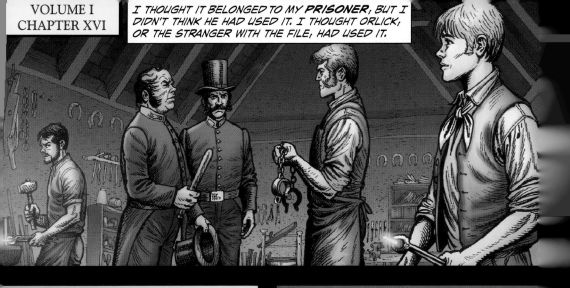

I THOUGHT IT BELONGED TO MY **PRISONER**, BUT I DIDN'T THINK HE HAD USED IT. I THOUGHT ORLICK, OR THE **STRANGER** WITH THE FILE, HAD USED IT.

THE POLICE WERE AT THE HOUSE FOR A WEEK OR TWO. THEY NEVER DISCOVERED WHO HAD HIT MY SISTER.

FOR A LONG TIME AFTER THEY HAD LEFT, MY SISTER LAY IN BED. SHE COULD NOT HEAR, SEE, SPEAK OR REMEMBER WELL.

FINALLY SHE CAME DOWNSTAIRS. SHE HAD TO WRITE DOWN WHAT SHE WANTED TO SAY.

SHE WAS CALM AND GENTLE.

WHEN MR WOPSLE'S **GREAT-AUNT** DIED, BIDDY CAME TO LIVE WITH US AND TO LOOK AFTER MY SISTER.

SHE WAS A GREAT HELP TO US, ESPECIALLY TO JOE, WHO WAS VERY SAD.

VOLUME I
CHAPTER XVII

I GOT USED TO BEING JOE'S **APPRENTICE**. I NOTICED THAT BIDDY NOW LOOKED BETTER. HER HAIR WAS BRIGHT AND HER HANDS WERE ALWAYS CLEAN.

SHE WAS COMMON – SHE COULD NOT BE LIKE ESTELLA – BUT SHE WAS PLEASANT AND KIND.

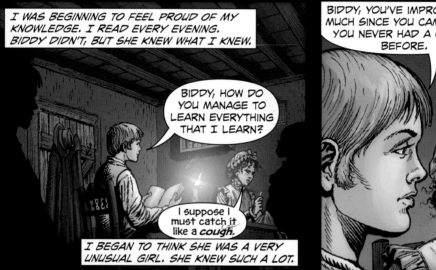

I WAS BEGINNING TO FEEL PROUD OF MY KNOWLEDGE. I READ EVERY EVENING. BIDDY DIDN'T, BUT SHE KNEW WHAT I KNEW.

BIDDY, HOW DO YOU MANAGE TO LEARN EVERYTHING THAT I LEARN?

I suppose I must catch it like a *cough*.

I BEGAN TO THINK SHE WAS A VERY UNUSUAL GIRL. SHE KNEW SUCH A LOT.

BIDDY, YOU'VE IMPROVED SO MUCH SINCE YOU CAME HERE! YOU NEVER HAD A CHANCE BEFORE.

I WAS YOUR FIRST TEACHER THOUGH, WASN'T I?

YES, YOU WERE. WE SHOULD TALK TOGETHER MORE, AS WE USED TO. LET'S HAVE A QUIET WALK ON THE **MARSHES** NEXT SUNDAY, AND A LONG TALK.

THAT SUNDAY AFTERNOON, WHILE JOE TOOK CARE OF MY SISTER, BIDDY AND I WENT OUT TOGETHER. I DECIDED TO TELL HER MY PLAN.

BIDDY, I WANT TO BE A **GENTLEMAN**.

YOU KNOW BEST, PIP, BUT AREN'T YOU HAPPIER AS YOU ARE?

BIDDY, I HATE MY WORK AND MY LIFE. I'LL BE **MISERABLE** UNLESS I CAN LEAD A VERY DIFFERENT SORT OF LIFE.

THAT'S A PITY!

IF I WAS HAPPY AT THE **FORGE**, JOE AND I COULD BE PARTNERS, AND YOU COULD BE MY WIFE. I WOULD BE GOOD ENOUGH FOR YOU, WOULDN'T I?

YES, I'M QUITE EASY TO PLEASE.

BUT INSTEAD, I'M UNHAPPY BECAUSE NOW I KNOW I'M COMMON.

THAT WASN'T A TRUE OR A NICE THING TO SAY. WHO SAID IT?

THE BEAUTIFUL YOUNG LADY AT MISS HAVISHAM'S. I ADMIRE HER SO MUCH, AND I WANT TO BE A **GENTLEMAN** BECAUSE OF HER.

DO YOU WANT TO MAKE HER ANGRY, OR TO MAKE HER LOVE YOU?

I DON'T KNOW.

45

I'M PLEASED YOU TOLD ME THIS.

BIDDY, I'LL ALWAYS TELL YOU EVERYTHING!

TILL YOU'RE A *GENTLEMAN.*

YOU KNOW I'LL NEVER BE ONE.

WE WALKED A LITTLE FARTHER, AND TALKED A LOT. I DECIDED THAT I SHOULD FORGET ESTELLA. BIDDY WAS NEVER **RUDE** TO ME. WHY DID I NOT LIKE HER MORE THAN ESTELLA?

BIDDY, I WISH YOU COULD MAKE ME BETTER.

I WISH I COULD!

I WISH I COULD FALL IN LOVE WITH YOU.

HAVE I HURT YOU BY SPEAKING SO OPENLY?

NOT AT ALL! DON'T WORRY.

IF I COULD FALL IN LOVE WITH YOU, *THAT* WOULD BE THE BEST THING FOR ME.

BUT YOU NEVER WILL, YOU SEE.

ONE SATURDAY NIGHT IN THE FOURTH YEAR OF MY WORK FOR JOE, A GROUP OF US SAT ROUND THE FIRE IN THE **PUB** AND LISTENED TO MR WOPSLE. HE READ TO US FROM THE NEWSPAPER. I NOTICED A STRANGE **GENTLEMAN** WHO WAS LOOKING AT US.

HE WENT AND STOOD BY THE FIRE. HE DID NOT RECOGNISE ME, BUT I RECOGNISED HIM. HE WAS THE GENTLEMAN I HAD MET ON THE STAIRS ON MY SECOND VISIT TO MISS HAVISHAM.

I BELIEVE THERE IS A **BLACKSMITH** HERE. HE'S CALLED JOE GARGERY. WHICH OF YOU IS HIM?

I AM.

IS YOUR **APPRENTICE** PIP HERE?

I'M HERE!

I WANT TO TALK TO YOU BOTH IN PRIVATE. IT WILL TAKE A LITTLE TIME. PERHAPS WE SHOULD GO TO YOUR HOUSE.

WE LEFT THE **PUB** AND WALKED HOME. WE SILENTLY WONDERED WHAT HE WAS GOING TO SAY.

MY NAME IS JAGGERS, AND I AM A LAWYER IN LONDON. I AM HERE ON UNUSUAL BUSINESS, WHICH I AM DOING FOR SOMEBODY ELSE.

JOSEPH GARGERY, I HAVE AN OFFER TO TAKE YOUR **APPRENTICE** AWAY.

WOULD YOU CANCEL HIS CONTRACT, IF HE WANTS YOU TO? WOULD YOU WANT ANYTHING FOR DOING SO?

NO. I WOULDN'T.

VERY WELL. I HAVE TO TELL YOU THAT PIP HAS GREAT **EXPECTATIONS.**

LATER, HE WILL OWN A BIG HOUSE. THE OWNER OF THIS HOUSE WANTS PIP TO LEAVE HIS PRESENT LIFE AND TO LEARN TO BE A **GENTLEMAN** – IN A WORD, A YOUNG MAN OF GREAT EXPECTATIONS.

MY DREAM HAD COME TRUE. MISS HAVISHAM WAS GOING TO MAKE ME RICH.

THE PERSON WHO INSTRUCTS ME HAS ASKED THAT YOU ALWAYS KEEP THE NAME PIP. DO YOU **OBJECT** TO THIS?

N-N-N-NO.

MY HEART WAS BEATING SO FAST I COULDN'T SPEAK PROPERLY.

THE NAME OF YOUR **BENEFACTOR** IS A SECRET AT THE MOMENT. THE PERSON WILL TELL YOU THEIR NAME, BUT I CANNOT SAY WHEN THEY WILL. IT MAY BE YEARS FROM NOW.

YOU MUST NOT TRY TO FIND OUT WHO YOUR BENEFACTOR IS. IF YOU THINK YOU KNOW, DO NOT SAY ANYTHING TO ANYONE. DO YOU OBJECT TO THIS CONDITION?

N-N-N-NO.

stuttering

YOUR BENEFACTOR HAS GIVEN ME SOME MONEY FOR YOUR EDUCATION. YOU MUST HAVE A BETTER EDUCATION FOR YOUR NEW POSITION IN LIFE.

I HAVE ALWAYS WANTED MORE EDUCATION.

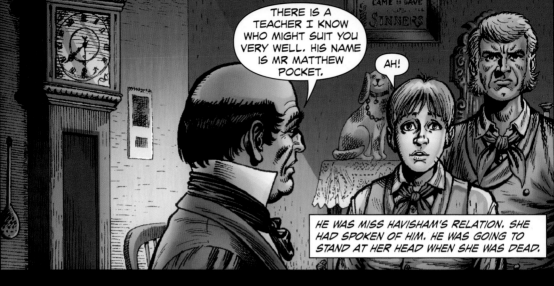

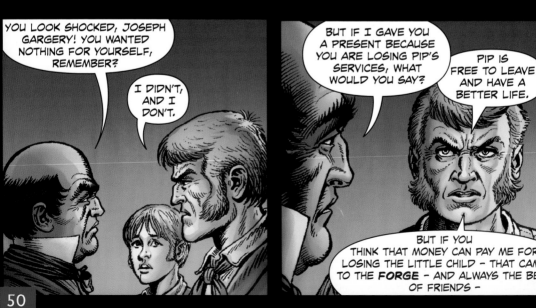

PIP'S A RICH **GENTLEMAN!**

I TOLD BIDDY AND JOE THEY MUST SAY NOTHING ABOUT MY **BENEFACTOR**. BIDDY SAID SHE WOULD BE VERY CAREFUL.

I WILL BE TOO, PIP.

BIDDY TRIED VERY HARD TO TELL MY SISTER WHAT HAD HAPPENED.

Pip ...

... property

I DON'T THINK MY SISTER UNDERSTOOD THE WORDS SHE REPEATED.

THAT NIGHT WHEN I OPENED THE WINDOW, I SAW JOE AND BIDDY OUTSIDE. I KNEW THAT THEY WERE TALKING ABOUT ME, BECAUSE I HEARD MY NAME.

IT WAS STRANGE THAT THIS FIRST NIGHT OF MY NEW LIFE WAS THE LONELIEST I HAD EVER HAD.

I WENT TO BED BUT I SLEPT UNEASILY IN IT. I NEVER SLEPT WELL IN IT AGAIN.

THE NEXT MORNING, JOE PUT THE CONTRACT FOR MY WORK IN THE FIRE. I FELT THAT I WAS FREE.

AFTER CHURCH, AND DINNER, I WENT FOR A WALK.

AS I PASSED THE CHURCH, I REMEMBERED THE *PRISONER* I HAD MET THERE. I FELT ASHAMED OF HELPING HIM. HE WAS PROBABLY IN A DISTANT COUNTRY NOW, AND WAS DEAD TO ME.

I WALKED OUT TO THE OLD *BATTERY*. I LAY DOWN TO THINK ABOUT ESTELLA AND FELL ASLEEP.

WHEN I WOKE UP, JOE WAS SITTING BESIDE ME.

I'VE ALWAYS WANTED TO BE A *GENTLEMAN*.

HAVE YOU?!

IT'S A PITY THAT YOU DIDN'T LEARN MORE IN OUR LESSONS, ISN'T IT?

I DON'T KNOW. I ONLY KNOW ABOUT MY WORK.

AFTER TEA, I TOOK BIDDY INTO OUR LITTLE GARDEN. I SAID I WANTED TO ASK HER TO DO SOMETHING FOR ME.

WILL YOU HELP JOE WITH HIS LEARNING AND HIS MANNERS?

OH! AREN'T HIS MANNERS GOOD ENOUGH THEN?

IF I MOVED JOE INTO HIGHER SOCIETY ...

HE MAY BE TOO PROUD TO LEAVE A PLACE IN SOCIETY THAT HE FILLS WELL AND WITH RESPECT.

I'M SORRY TO SEE YOU LIKE THIS, BIDDY.

YOU'RE *JEALOUS* OF ME.

IF YOU THINK SO!

I'M SORRY TO SEE THIS IN YOU – IT'S A BAD SIDE OF HUMAN NATURE.

I WON'T ASK YOU TO DO ANYTHING.

IN THE MORNING I FORGAVE BIDDY, AND WE DID NOT SPEAK OF JOE. I WENT INTO TOWN TO ORDER SOME NEW CLOTHES.

WHEN I HAD ORDERED EVERYTHING, I WENT TO PUMBLECHOOK'S.

MY DEAR FRIEND! WELL DONE! WELL DONE!

I'M SO PROUD THAT I HELPED THIS TO HAPPEN!

REMEMBER THAT THAT IS A SECRET.

MY DEAR YOUNG FRIEND, YOU MUST BE HUNGRY; YOU MUST BE TIRED.

... AND TO YOUR SISTER, WHO **BROUGHT** YOU **UP!**

TO HER HEALTH!

AH! THAT'S GOOD OF YOU, SIR!

ON FRIDAY I COLLECTED MY NEW CLOTHES. I PUT THEM ON AND WENT TO VISIT MISS HAVISHAM. SARAH POCKET CAME TO THE GATE.

YOU? WHAT DO YOU WANT?

I'M GOING TO LONDON, MISS POCKET, AND I WANT TO SAY GOODBYE TO MISS HAVISHAM.

SHE TOOK ME UP TO MISS HAVISHAM.

DON'T GO, SARAH.

WELL, PIP?

I'M GOING TO LONDON TOMORROW, AND AM HERE TO SAY GOODBYE TO YOU.

YOU LOOK VERY FINE.

I HAVE COME INTO SUCH GOOD **FORTUNE**, MISS HAVISHAM, AND I AM SO **GRATEFUL!**

MR JAGGERS HAS TOLD ME, PIP.

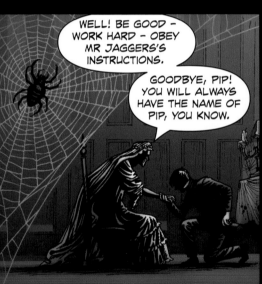

WELL! BE GOOD – WORK HARD – OBEY MR JAGGERS'S INSTRUCTIONS.

GOODBYE, PIP! YOU WILL ALWAYS HAVE THE NAME OF PIP, YOU KNOW.

ON MY LAST EVENING, I WORE MY NEW CLOTHES FOR JOE AND BIDDY. WE ALL PRETENDED TO BE HAPPY, BUT WE WERE VERY LOW. I HAD TO LEAVE AT FIVE THE NEXT MORNING. I HAD TOLD JOE THAT I WANTED TO GO ALONE.

AFTER A QUICK BREAKFAST, I PICKED UP MY BAG AND WALKED OUT.

HOOROAR!

IT WAS EASIER TO LEAVE THAN I HAD EXPECTED.

BUT THE VILLAGE WAS VERY PEACEFUL, AND EVERYTHING BEYOND IT WAS SO UNKNOWN, THAT I STARTED TO CRY. AFTER I HAD CRIED I FELT MORE SORRY.

I KNEW THAT I WAS **UNGRATEFUL.**

WHEN I WAS ON THE COACH, I THOUGHT OF GOING BACK.

I COULD HAVE ANOTHER EVENING AT HOME AND LEAVE JOE AND BIDDY IN A BETTER WAY. BUT THEN IT WAS TOO LATE AND TOO FAR TO GO BACK.

VOLUME II
CHAPTER I

WE REACHED LONDON AT MIDDAY. IT FRIGHTENED ME. IT WAS HUGE, AND QUITE UGLY AND DIRTY.

MR JAGGERS HAD SENT ME HIS ADDRESS. IT WAS LITTLE BRITAIN. I TOOK A COACH THERE AND SOON ARRIVED IN A DARK STREET.

IS MR JAGGERS AT HOME?

NO, HE'S IN **COURT.**

ARE YOU MR. PIP?

YES.

MR JAGGERS WOULD LIKE YOU TO WAIT IN HIS ROOM. HE'LL BE BACK AS SOON AS HE CAN.

MR JAGGERS'S ROOM WAS DARK AND UNPLEASANT.

I WAITED THERE UNTIL I COULD BEAR IT NO LONGER. I TOLD THE **CLERK** THAT I WAS GOING OUT FOR SOME FRESH AIR. I WALKED PAST A STONE BUILDING. SOMEONE TOLD ME IT WAS NEWGATE **PRISON.**

WHEN I RETURNED TO LITTLE BRITAIN, OTHER PEOPLE WERE WAITING FOR MR JAGGERS. AT LAST HE CAME BACK AND THE OTHER PEOPLE RUSHED TOWARDS HIM.

I HAVE NOTHING TO SAY TO YOU. I DON'T WANT TO KNOW ANY MORE.

HAVE YOU PAID WEMMICK?

YES, SIR.

WHAT ABOUT ME, SIR?

IF YOU COME AND BOTHER ME, I WON'T DO ANYTHING FOR YOU.

HAVE YOU PAID WEMMICK?

OH YES, SIR!

MR JAGGERS TOOK ME INTO HIS ROOM. WHILE HE HAD LUNCH, HE TOLD ME WHAT HE HAD ARRANGED FOR ME. I HAD TO GO TO BARNARD'S INN, TO YOUNG MR POCKET'S ROOMS. I HAD TO STAY THERE UNTIL MONDAY, AND THEN GO WITH HIM TO HIS FATHER'S HOUSE.

HE TOLD ME HOW MUCH MONEY I WOULD GET EVERY MONTH.

YOU ARE GETTING A LOT OF MONEY, BUT I WILL BE CHECKING HOW YOU SPEND IT.

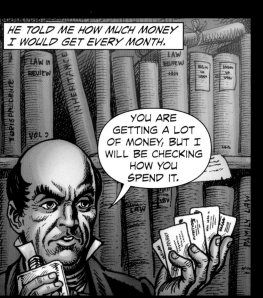

WEMMICK WALKED WITH ME TO MR POCKET'S.

HE WON'T SPEAK TO ANY OF YOU.

VOLUME II
CHAPTER II

WE SOON LEFT THE PEOPLE AT MR JAGGERS'S DOOR, AND WALKED ON SIDE BY SIDE.

SO, YOU'VE NEVER BEEN TO LONDON BEFORE? I WAS NEW HERE ONCE. STRANGE TO THINK SO NOW!

IS IT A VERY BAD PLACE?

PEOPLE MAY **ROB** YOU OR MURDER YOU IN LONDON, BUT THEY MAY DO THAT ANYWHERE.

AT LAST WE ARRIVED AT BARNARD'S **INN**. IT WAS THE DIRTIEST AND DARKEST GROUP OF BUILDINGS I HAD EVER SEEN.

MR WEMMICK LED ME UP SOME STAIRS TO A SET OF ROOMS ON THE TOP FLOOR.

HE DIDN'T THINK YOU WOULD COME SO SOON. DO YOU WANT ME ANY MORE?

NO, THANK YOU.

AS I KEEP THE MONEY, WE'LL PROBABLY MEET QUITE OFTEN. GOODBYE.

I WAS GETTING VERY BORED, BUT THEN I HEARD **FOOTSTEPS** ON THE STAIRS.

MR PIP? I'M EXTREMELY SORRY. I WENT OUT TO BUY YOU SOME FRUIT FOR AFTER DINNER.

LET ME TAKE THESE BAGS FROM YOU. **GOOD HEAVENS**, YOU'RE THE BOY IN THE GARDEN!

AND YOU'RE THE **PALE** YOUNG **GENTLEMAN!**

HOW FUNNY THAT IT'S YOU!

HOW FUNNY THAT IT'S YOU! WELL, IT'S ALL FORGOTTEN NOW. I HOPE YOU'LL **FORGIVE** ME FOR HITTING YOU SO HARD.

I REALISED THAT MR HERBERT HAD FORGOTTEN WHAT HAD HAPPENED.

MISS HAVISHAM HAD INVITED ME FOR A VISIT TO SEE IF I WOULD BE A GOOD HUSBAND FOR ESTELLA. BUT SHE DIDN'T LIKE ME.

WERE YOU DISAPPOINTED?

NO! SHE'S **HORRIBLE**.

MISS HAVISHAM?

WELL, HER TOO, BUT I MEANT ESTELLA. MISS HAVISHAM HAS **BROUGHT** HER **UP** TO TAKE **REVENGE** ON MEN.

HOW IS SHE RELATED TO MISS HAVISHAM?

SHE ISN'T. SHE'S **ADOPTED** BY HER.

WHY DOES MISS HAVISHAM WANT REVENGE ON MEN?

HEAVENS, MR PIP! DON'T YOU KNOW? IT'S QUITE A LONG STORY. I'LL TELL IT TO YOU AT DINNER.

MR JAGGERS HAS SUGGESTED MY FATHER AS YOUR TEACHER. MY FATHER IS RELATED TO MISS HAVISHAM, AND MR JAGGERS KNEW ABOUT HIM THROUGH HER. MR JAGGERS IS MISS HAVISHAM'S LAWYER.

I TOLD HIM WHAT HAD HAPPENED TO ME. I SAID THAT I WAS **FORBIDDEN** TO ASK WHO MY **BENEFACTOR** WAS.

I HAVE GROWN UP AS A **BLACKSMITH** IN THE COUNTRY, SO MY MANNERS AREN'T VERY GOOD. PLEASE TELL ME WHEN I DO THINGS WRONGLY.

WITH PLEASURE.

PLEASE CALL ME HERBERT.

THANK YOU. MY NAME'S PHILIP.

I DON'T LIKE THE NAME PHILIP. COULD I CALL YOU HANDEL INSTEAD?

THERE'S A LOVELY PIECE OF MUSIC ABOUT A BLACKSMITH BY HANDEL.

I'D LIKE THAT VERY MUCH.

NOW, MY DEAR HANDEL, DINNER IS SERVED. PLEASE SIT AT THE TOP OF THE TABLE AS YOU ARE PAYING FOR DINNER.

I WOULDN'T DO SO, SO HE SAT AT THE TOP. AFTER WE HAD EATEN A LITTLE, I REMINDED HIM OF HIS PROMISE TO TELL ME ABOUT MISS HAVISHAM.

MISS HAVISHAM'S MOTHER DIED WHEN SHE WAS A BABY. HER FATHER WAS A COUNTRY **GENTLEMAN.** HE GAVE HER EVERYTHING SHE WANTED. HE WAS VERY RICH AND VERY PROUD, AND SO WAS SHE.

WAS SHE AN ONLY CHILD?

SINCE THEN SHE HAS NEVER SEEN **DAYLIGHT**.

I'VE FORGOTTEN ONE THING: THE MAN SHE WAS GOING TO MARRY PLANNED EVERYTHING WITH HER BROTHER. THEY SHARED THE MONEY BETWEEN THEM.

WHAT HAPPENED TO THEM?

THEY FELL INTO SHAME AND RUIN. I DON'T KNOW IF THEY ARE STILL ALIVE.

WE BEGAN TO TALK ABOUT OTHER THINGS. HERBERT TOLD ME ABOUT HIS PLANS FOR MAKING MONEY.

YOU HAVE TO WAIT UNTIL THE TIME IS RIGHT. THEN YOU MOVE IN QUICKLY AND MAKE YOUR MONEY.

AS I LISTENED TO HERBERT'S PLANS, IT SEEMED AS IF I HAD LEFT JOE AND BIDDY MANY MONTHS BEFORE.

ON MONDAY MORNING, HERBERT AND I WENT TO THE **COUNTING-HOUSE** WHERE HE WORKED. AFTER LUNCH, WE WENT TO VISIT MR MATTHEW POCKET.

AFTER WE GOT OUT OF THE COACH, WE WALKED A LITTLE WAY TO HIS HOUSE. WE OPENED A GATE AND WENT INTO A LITTLE GARDEN NEAR THE RIVER. MR POCKET'S CHILDREN WERE PLAYING THERE.

MR POCKET CAME OUT TO MEET ME.

BELINDA, I HOPE YOU'VE WELCOMED MR PIP?

Y-Y-YES ...

I FOUND OUT A FEW HOURS LATER THAT MRS POCKET WAS THE DAUGHTER OF A RICH MAN. HE HAD WANTED HER TO MARRY ANOTHER RICH MAN. HOWEVER, SHE HAD MET MR POCKET AND HAD MARRIED HIM WITHOUT HER FATHER'S KNOWLEDGE.

MR POCKET TOOK ME INTO THE HOUSE AND SHOWED ME MY ROOM. THEN HE INTRODUCED ME TO TWO OTHER PEOPLE IN THE HOUSE: DRUMMLE AND STARTOP.

AT DINNER I REALISED THAT THE SERVANTS WERE THE PEOPLE IN THE HOUSE WHO HAD THE POWER. THEY ALLOWED THE POCKETS GOOD FOOD, BUT THEY HAD MUCH BETTER FOOD THEMSELVES.

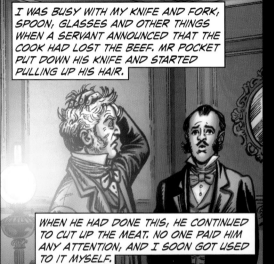

I WAS BUSY WITH MY KNIFE AND FORK, SPOON, GLASSES AND OTHER THINGS WHEN A SERVANT ANNOUNCED THAT THE COOK HAD LOST THE BEEF. MR POCKET PUT DOWN HIS KNIFE AND STARTED PULLING UP HIS HAIR.

WHEN HE HAD DONE THIS, HE CONTINUED TO CUT UP THE MEAT. NO ONE PAID HIM ANY ATTENTION, AND I SOON GOT USED TO IT MYSELF.

AFTER DINNER, A SERVANT CALLED SOPHIA TOLD MR POCKET THAT THE COOK WAS DRUNK AND WAS LYING ON THE KITCHEN FLOOR.

SOPHIA'S MAKING TROUBLE! DO YOU BELIEVE HER? IS MY OPINION OF HER NOT IMPORTANT?

GOODNIGHT, MR PIP.

VOLUME II
CHAPTER V

TWO OR THREE DAYS LATER, MR POCKET AND I HAD A LONG TALK. MR JAGGERS HAD TOLD HIM THAT I NEEDED A GOOD EDUCATION. MR POCKET ADVISED ME TO GO TO DIFFERENT PLACES IN LONDON TO LEARN VARIOUS THINGS. HE WOULD BE THE DIRECTOR OF ALL MY STUDIES.

I REALISED THAT I WOULD HAVE A MORE VARIED LIFE IF I LIVED IN BARNARD'S *INN*. MR POCKET DID NOT MIND THIS ARRANGEMENT, BUT I HAD TO ASK PERMISSION FROM MR JAGGERS.

I WENT TO LITTLE BRITAIN TO TELL MR JAGGERS MY IDEA.

IF I COULD BUY SOME FURNITURE, I'D FEEL AT HOME THERE.

REALLY?! SO HOW MUCH MONEY DO YOU WANT?

FIFTY POUNDS?

OH, NOT SO MUCH.

FIVE POUNDS?

OH, MORE THAN THAT.

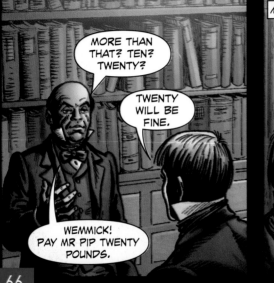

MORE THAN THAT? TEN? TWENTY?

TWENTY WILL BE FINE.

WEMMICK! PAY MR PIP TWENTY POUNDS.

MR JAGGERS LEFT THE ROOM.

I DON'T UNDERSTAND MR JAGGERS.

HE'D BE PLEASED TO HEAR IT.

HE DOESN'T WANT YOU TO UNDERSTAND HIM. IT'S NOT PERSONAL. HE ALWAYS WORKS LIKE THAT.

WHO ARE THEY?

THEY ARE TWO FAMOUS CLIENTS OF OURS.

THIS ONE MURDERED HIS **MASTER**. HE WAS **HANGED**.

HE HAD THIS MADE ESPECIALLY FOR ME!

WHAT ABOUT THE OTHER ONE? WAS HE HANGED TOO?

YES, HE WAS. HE BOUGHT ME THIS THE DAY BEFORE HE DIED.

DOES ALL YOUR **JEWELLERY** COME FROM PEOPLE LIKE THEM?

OH YES. I ALWAYS TAKE THE PRESENTS THEY GIVE ME.

IF YOU EVER WANT TO VISIT ME AT HOME IN WALWORTH, I COULD OFFER YOU A BED FOR THE NIGHT.

I HAVE TWO OR THREE INTERESTING THINGS YOU MIGHT LIKE TO SEE.

I WOULD BE VERY HAPPY TO COME.

HAVE YOU HAD DINNER WITH MR JAGGERS YET?

NOT YET.

WHEN YOU DO, LOOK AT HIS **HOUSEKEEPER**. YOU'LL SEE A WILD ANIMAL THAT HE'S **TAMED**.

VOLUME II
CHAPTER VI

A FEW WEEKS LATER, I WROTE A NOTE TO MR WEMMICK. I SUGGESTED THAT I WENT HOME WITH HIM ONE EVENING. HE REPLIED THAT IT WOULD GIVE HIM MUCH PLEASURE, AND HE WOULD EXPECT ME AT HIS OFFICE AT SIX O'CLOCK.

I'VE GOT MY OLD FATHER AT MY PLACE. DO YOU MIND?

NOT AT ALL.

SO, YOU HAVEN'T HAD DINNER WITH MR JAGGERS YET? I EXPECT YOU'LL HAVE AN INVITATION TOMORROW. HE'S GOING TO INVITE YOUR FRIENDS TOO.

AFTER A LONG WALK, WE ARRIVED IN WALWORTH, AT MR WEMMICK'S HOUSE.

I MADE THAT. IT LOOKS PRETTY, DOESN'T IT?

AFTER I'VE **CROSSED** THE BRIDGE, I PULL IT UP.

HE PULLED UP THE BRIDGE VERY PROUDLY AND TIED IT UP.

AT NINE O'CLOCK EVERY NIGHT, THE **GUN FIRES**. THERE IT IS!

I MADE EVERYTHING HERE. I LIKE DOING IT. IT MAKES ME FORGET MY WORK AT NEWGATE, AND IT MAKES MY OLD FATHER HAPPY.

YOU WOULDN'T MIND MEETING HIM, WOULD YOU?

WE WENT INTO THE CASTLE. A VERY OLD MAN WAS SITTING BY THE FIRE. HE WAS CHEERFUL AND COMFORTABLE, BUT VERY **DEAF**.

HERE'S MR PIP, FATHER. NOD AT HIM, MR PIP. HE LIKES THAT.

ALL RIGHT, JOHN, ALL RIGHT.

WE SAT DOWN TO HAVE A DRINK.

IT'S TAKEN ME YEARS TO MAKE THE HOUSE PERFECT.

DOES MR. JAGGERS LIKE IT?

HE'S NEVER SEEN IT, OR HEARD OF IT.

I DON'T SPEAK ABOUT THE CASTLE AT THE OFFICE AND I'D LIKE YOU TO DO THE SAME. IT'S NEARLY TIME FOR **GUN-FIRE**. THE OLD MAN LIKES IT.

INSIDE THE CASTLE THE OLD MAN WAS HEATING THE **POKER**. WEMMICK TOOK IT FROM HIM AND WENT UP TO THE **GUN**.

THE GUN WENT OFF LOUDLY AND SHOOK THE HOUSE.

BANG

I HEARD IT!

OUR MEAL WAS EXCELLENT, AND SO WAS MY LITTLE BEDROOM.

MR WEMMICK GOT UP EARLY IN THE MORNING.

WE HAD BREAKFAST AND AT HALF PAST EIGHT LEFT FOR LITTLE BRITAIN.

AS MR WEMMICK HAD SAID, MR JAGGERS ASKED ME AND MY FRIENDS TO DINNER THE NEXT DAY.

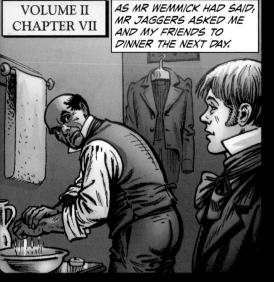

THE **HOUSEKEEPER** BROUGHT THE FIRST DISH TO THE TABLE. SHE WAS QUITE TALL, EXTREMELY **PALE**, WITH LARGE EYES AND LONG HAIR. HER EYES WERE ALWAYS FIXED ON MR JAGGERS.

WE BEGAN TO TALK ABOUT ROWING. WE MADE FUN OF DRUMMLE FOR COMING LAST. DRUMMLE SHOWED US HIS ARM TO SHOW HOW STRONG IT WAS. WE ALL BEGAN TO SHOW OUR ARMS.

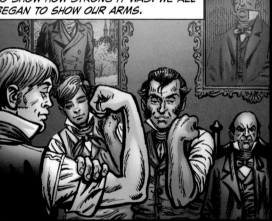

AT THAT TIME THE HOUSEKEEPER WAS CLEARING THE TABLE. MR JAGGERS SUDDENLY PUT HIS HAND DOWN ON TOP OF HERS.

IF YOU TALK OF STRENGTH, I'LL SHOW YOU AN ARM. MOLLY, LET THEM SEE YOUR ARM.

Master, don't.

MOLLY; LET THEM SEE *BOTH* YOUR ARMS. SHOW THEM!

VERY FEW MEN HAVE **WRISTS** AS POWERFUL AS THIS WOMAN'S.

THAT'S ALL, MOLLY. YOU CAN GO.

WE CARRIED ON TALKING AND DRINKING, AND LEFT AT HALF PAST NINE.

ABOUT A MONTH LATER, I RECEIVED A LETTER.

My dear Mr Pip,

Mr Gargery has asked me to tell you that he is going to London and would like to see you. He will call at Barnard's Hotel on Tuesday morning at nine o'clock.

Your sister is the same as when you left. We talk about you in the kitchen every night and wonder what you are doing.

Yours,
Biddy

JOE WAS COMING THE NEXT DAY. I DIDN'T WANT TO SEE HIM, BUT I HAD TO.

I GOT UP EARLY THE NEXT MORNING AND MADE THE ROOMS IN BARNARD'S *INN* LOOK AS PLEASANT AS I COULD. SOON I HEARD JOE ON THE STAIRS. I KNEW IT WAS HIM BY THE WAY HE CLIMBED THEM. AT LAST HE STOPPED OUTSIDE OUR DOOR AND KNOCKED ON IT QUIETLY.

≥knock!≤

JOE, HOW ARE YOU, JOE?

PIP, HOW ARE YOU, PIP?

IT'S GOOD TO SEE YOU, JOE. GIVE ME YOUR HAT.

YOU'VE GROWN! AND BECOME A **GENTLEMAN.**

AND YOU, JOE, LOOK WONDERFULLY WELL.

AS WE ARE ALONE, SIR ...

JOE, HOW CAN YOU CALL ME SIR?

AS WE ARE ALONE, I'LL TELL YOU WHY I'M HERE. I WAS AT THE **PUB** A FEW DAYS AGO AND **PUMBLECHOOK** CAME UP TO ME. HE SAID THAT MISS HAVISHAM WANTED TO SPEAK TO ME.

SO THE NEXT DAY I WENT TO SEE HER.

MISS HAVISHAM?

YES. SHE TOLD ME TO TELL YOU THAT ESTELLA HAS COME HOME AND WOULD LIKE TO SEE YOU.

THAT'S WHAT I HAD TO SAY, SIR. I WISH YOU VERY WELL.

YOU'RE NOT GOING NOW, JOE?

YES, I AM.

PIP, DEAR OLD **CHAP**, YOU AND I SHOULDN'T BE TOGETHER IN LONDON.

I'M WRONG IN THESE CLOTHES, AND I'M WRONG OUT OF THE **FORGE**. SO GOODBYE, DEAR PIP, GOODBYE!

HE TOUCHED ME GENTLY ON THE HEAD AND LEFT.

VOLUME II
CHAPTER IX

I HAD TO GO BACK TO OUR VILLAGE THE NEXT DAY. I KNEW THAT I SHOULD STAY AT JOE'S, BUT I BEGAN TO MAKE EXCUSES FOR STAYING AT THE BLUE **BOAR**.

THE NEXT DAY I ARRIVED AT THE COACH STATION EARLY. AT THAT TIME, **PRISONERS** USED TO TRAVEL DOWN TO THE SHIPS BY COACH. I FOUND THAT TWO WERE IN MY COACH.

YOU DON'T MIND THEM, HANDEL?

OH NO! I DON'T MIND THEM.

THERE THEY ARE.

THE TWO PRISONERS HAD **LEG-IRONS** ON. ONE OF THEM WAS TALLER AND FATTER THAN THE OTHER. I RECOGNISED HIM IMMEDIATELY. HE WAS THE MAN WHO HAD SHOWED ME THE **FILE** AT THE **PUB**!

THE WEATHER WAS **MISERABLY** COLD AND IT MADE US ALL TIRED. I FELL ASLEEP WHILE I WAS WONDERING WHETHER TO GIVE THE PRISONER SOME MONEY. I REMEMBERED THE TWO POUNDS HE HAD GIVEN ME.

I WOKE UP SUDDENLY. THE **PRISONERS** WERE WHISPERING TO EACH OTHER.

TWO ONE POUND NOTES.

HOW DID HE GET THEM?

I DON'T KNOW. HE HAD HIDDEN THEM SOMEWHERE. HE SAID TO ME, 'ARE YOU GETTING OUT?' I SAID I WAS. HE ASKED ME TO FIND THE BOY THAT HAD FED HIM AND KEPT HIS SECRET AND TO GIVE HIM THESE TWO ONE-POUND NOTES. I SAID I WOULD, AND I DID.

DID HE KNOW YOU?

NO, WE WERE ON DIFFERENT SHIPS. HE ESCAPED AGAIN, AND WAS SENT TO **PRISON** FOR LIFE.

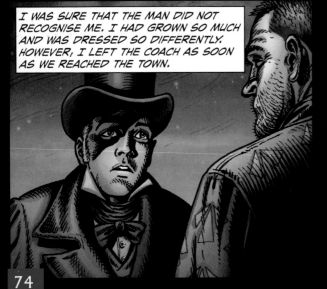

I WAS SURE THAT THE MAN DID NOT RECOGNISE ME. I HAD GROWN SO MUCH AND WAS DRESSED SO DIFFERENTLY. HOWEVER, I LEFT THE COACH AS SOON AS WE REACHED THE TOWN.

THE PRISONERS STAYED ON THE COACH, BUT I WAS STILL AFRAID WHEN I WALKED ON TO THE BLUE **BOAR**.

I WAS UP EARLY IN THE MORNING. IT WAS TOO EARLY TO GO TO MISS HAVISHAM'S SO I WENT FOR A WALK IN THE COUNTRY. I THOUGHT ABOUT MISS HAVISHAM'S PLANS FOR ESTELLA AND ME.

I ARRIVED AT THE GATE TO MISS HAVISHAM'S AND RANG THE **BELL**. THEN I TURNED ROUND.

ORLICK!

AH, YOUNG **MASTER**, THINGS HAVE CHANGED AROUND HERE. BUT COME IN. I MUSTN'T KEEP THE GATE OPEN.

HAVE YOU LEFT THE **FORGE**?

DOES THIS LOOK LIKE THE FORGE?

ORLICK RANG A BELL AND LEFT ME. I CLIMBED THE STAIRS IN THE DARK. I KNOCKED IN MY OLD WAY ON MISS HAVISHAM'S DOOR.

tap-tap

PIP'S KNOCK. COME IN, PIP.

THERE WAS A LADY NEXT TO MISS HAVISHAM THAT I HAD NEVER SEEN BEFORE.

COME IN, PIP. HOW ARE YOU? SO YOU KISS MY HAND AS IF I WERE A QUEEN?

I HEARD YOU WISHED TO SEE ME, SO I CAME IMMEDIATELY.

WELL?

THE LADY THAT I HAD NEVER SEEN BEFORE LOOKED AT ME. I SAW THAT SHE WAS ...

... ESTELLA.

SHE WAS SO CHANGED, SO MUCH MORE BEAUTIFUL, THAT I BECAME THE POOR, COMMON BOY AGAIN. I SAID I WAS VERY PLEASED TO SEE HER AND THAT I HAD **LOOKED FORWARD TO** IT FOR A LONG, LONG TIME.

DO YOU THINK SHE HAS CHANGED MUCH, PIP?

YES, BUT I CAN STILL SEE THE OLD ...

WHAT? THE OLD ESTELLA? SHE WAS PROUD AND **RUDE.** DON'T YOU REMEMBER?

THAT WAS LONG AGO, AND I DIDN'T KNOW MUCH THEN.

ESTELLA SMILED CALMLY. SHE SAID SHE WAS SURE I HAD BEEN RIGHT. SHE HAD BEEN VERY UNPLEASANT.

MISS HAVISHAM SENT US OUT TO THE GARDEN. I SHOWED ESTELLA WHERE SHE HAD GIVEN ME MY MEAT AND DRINK.

I DON'T REMEMBER.

YOU DON'T REMEMBER THAT YOU MADE ME CRY?

NO.

ESTELLA, NOT REMEMBERING, AND NOT MINDING AT ALL, MADE ME CRY AGAIN INSIDE.

I HAVE NO HEART – IF THAT HAS ANYTHING TO DO WITH MY MEMORY. I HAVE NO SOFTNESS, NO FEELING.

WHAT DID I RECOGNISE WHEN SHE LOOKED AT ME? WAS IT SOMETHING I HAD SEEN IN MISS HAVISHAM? NO. WHERE HAD I SEEN IT THEN?

WE WENT BACK INTO THE HOUSE WHERE MISS HAVISHAM WAS WAITING FOR ME IN HER CHAIR. I PUSHED HER AROUND, AS IN THE OLD DAYS. I WAS SURPRISED TO HEAR THAT MR JAGGERS WAS COMING TO DINNER.

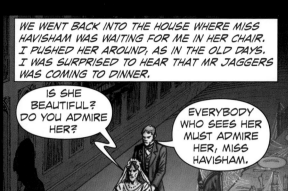

IS SHE BEAUTIFUL? DO YOU ADMIRE HER?

EVERYBODY WHO SEES HER MUST ADMIRE HER, MISS HAVISHAM.

LOVE HER, LOVE HER, LOVE HER!

IF SHE LIKES YOU, LOVE HER. IF SHE HURTS YOU, LOVE HER. I **ADOPTED** HER AND **BROUGHT** HER **UP** TO BE LOVED.

LOVE HER!

SHE GAVE A WILD **CRY** AND ROSE UP IN THE CHAIR. AS I PULLED HER DOWN AGAIN, I SAW MR JAGGERS. MISS HAVISHAM HAD SEEN HIM TOO, AND TRIED TO CALM HERSELF.

SHE SENT US DOWN TO OUR DINNER. SHE NEVER ATE OR DRANK IN FRONT OF PEOPLE. SHE WALKED AROUND THE HOUSE AT NIGHT AND ATE THEN.

SIR, MAY I ASK YOU A QUESTION?

ESTELLA'S NAME, IS IT HAVISHAM, OR –

IT IS HAVISHAM.

AFTER DINNER WE WENT UP TO MISS HAVISHAM'S ROOM AND PLAYED CARDS. IT WAS ARRANGED THAT I WOULD MEET ESTELLA'S COACH WHEN SHE CAME TO LONDON.

THEN I LEFT.

MR JAGGERS WAS IN THE ROOM NEXT TO MINE AT THE BLUE **BOAR**. FAR INTO THE NIGHT, I HEARD MISS HAVISHAM'S WORDS, 'LOVE HER, LOVE HER, LOVE HER!' I FELT **GRATEFUL** THAT SHE WAS MEANT FOR ME. I NO LONGER THOUGHT THAT THERE WAS ANYTHING WRONG IN STAYING AWAY FROM JOE. I KNEW ESTELLA THOUGHT HE WAS COMMON.

THE NEXT MORNING I TOLD MR JAGGERS THAT ORLICK WAS NOT THE RIGHT SORT OF MAN FOR A POSITION OF TRUST AT MISS HAVISHAM'S.

OF COURSE HE'S NOT THE RIGHT SORT OF MAN, PIP. THE MAN WHO FILLS A POSITION OF TRUST IS NEVER THE RIGHT SORT OF MAN.

I'LL GO ROUND NOW AND TELL HIM TO LEAVE.

I WAS RATHER SHOCKED BY THE SPEED OF HIS RESPONSE BUT HE INSISTED.

JAGGERS AND I TOOK THE MIDDAY COACH BACK TO LONDON. AS SOON AS I ARRIVED I WENT TO BARNARD'S INN.

MY DEAR HERBERT, I HAVE SOMETHING VERY IMPORTANT TO TELL YOU.

I LOVE ESTELLA.

I KNOW.

HOW DO YOU KNOW? I NEVER TOLD YOU.

TOLD ME! WHEN YOU TOLD ME ABOUT YOURSELF YOU SAID THAT YOU BEGAN LOVING HER THE FIRST TIME YOU SAW HER.

I SAW HER YESTERDAY, AND NOW I LOVE HER TWICE AS MUCH.

IT'S LUCKY THEN THAT YOU ARE GOING TO MARRY HER.

AND NOW, HANDEL, I WANT TO TELL YOU SOMETHING.

I'M IN LOVE, BUT IT'S A SECRET. HER NAME'S CLARA.

SHE DOESN'T COME FROM A RICH FAMILY. HER FATHER USED TO BUY FOOD FOR PASSENGER SHIPS.

HE'S ILL NOW. I'VE NEVER MET HIM BECAUSE HE STAYS IN HIS ROOM.

I'VE HEARD HIM THOUGH. HE SHOUTS AND HITS THE FLOOR WITH SOMETHING!

HE LAUGHED, AND TOLD ME THAT WHEN HE HAD MONEY, HE WAS GOING TO MARRY THIS YOUNG LADY.

WE WARMLY SHOOK HANDS UPON OUR SECRETS, AND WENT TO THE THEATRE TO SEE MR WOPSLE. HE WAS NOW AN ACTOR AND WAS PERFORMING IN HAMLET IN LONDON.

AFTER THE PLAY I WONDERED WHETHER I WAS GOING TO PLAY HAMLET TO MISS HAVISHAM'S GHOST.

I RETURNED TO THE COACH STATION WITH THREE MORE HOURS TO WAIT. I THOUGHT ABOUT ESTELLA ALL THE TIME.

I WAS STILL SHAKING THE **PRISON DUST** FROM MY CLOTHES WHEN I SAW HER FACE AT THE COACH WINDOW.

STAGE COACH
CHEAPSIDE STATION 12 ESTABLISH 1792

WINES NOTED ALES BOTTLE AND CASK INN

E. COOKE.
PLUMBER
ESTIMATES GIVEN
63

VOLUME II
CHAPTER XIV

I'M GOING TO RICHMOND. YOU HAVE TO TAKE ME THERE AND PAY FOR IT FROM MY PURSE. WE MUST OBEY OUR INSTRUCTIONS.

WILL YOU REST HERE FOR A FEW MINUTES?

YES, I HAVE TO REST A LITTLE AND DRINK SOME TEA. YOU HAVE TO TAKE CARE OF ME.

HER WORDS HURT ME. SHE WAS WITH ME ONLY BECAUSE SHE HAD TO BE.

WHERE ARE YOU GOING TO IN RICHMOND?

I'M GOING TO LIVE WITH A LADY THERE. SHE'S GOING TO TAKE ME AROUND AND INTRODUCE ME TO PEOPLE.

HOW ARE YOU DOING WITH MR POCKET?

IT'S QUITE PLEASANT THERE. AS PLEASANT AS IT CAN BE - AWAY FROM YOU.

YOU'RE SO SILLY! YOUR FRIEND MR MATTHEW IS, I BELIEVE, BETTER THAN THE REST OF HIS FAMILY.

THE OTHERS WRITE TO MISS HAVISHAM ABOUT YOU. THEY SAY ALL KINDS OF UNTRUE THINGS ABOUT YOU.

YOU DON'T REALISE HOW MUCH THEY HATE YOU.

THEY SUFFER SO MUCH!

IT GIVES ME SUCH SATISFACTION TO SEE THEM UNHAPPY.

AFTER TEA WE GOT INTO OUR COACH AND DROVE AWAY.

WHAT'S THAT PLACE?

NEWGATE PRISON.

WHAT AWFUL PEOPLE!

WE ARRIVED IN RICHMOND, AT A DULL OLD HOUSE.

GOODNIGHT.

I STOOD AND LOOKED AT THE HOUSE. IF I LIVED THERE WITH HER, I WOULD BE SO HAPPY! BUT I KNEW THAT I WAS NEVER HAPPY WITH HER, ALWAYS MISERABLE.

I HAD BEGUN TO NOTICE THE EFFECT OF MY **EXPECTATIONS** ON MYSELF AND THOSE AROUND ME. IT WAS NOT GOOD. HERBERT WAS SPENDING TOO MUCH.

WE BEGAN TO HAVE MORE AND MORE DEBTS, AND SOMETIMES WE RECEIVED THREATENING LETTERS.

MY DEAR HERBERT, WE ARE NOT DOING WELL. WE NEED TO LOOK AT OUR **AFFAIRS**.

WE ALWAYS GOT GREAT SATISFACTION FROM DOING THIS. I FELT LIKE A FIRST-CLASS MAN OF BUSINESS.

slide

IT'S FOR YOU, HANDEL. I HOPE THERE IS NOTHING WRONG.

THE LETTER TOLD ME THAT MRS J. GARGERY HAD DIED. I WAS ASKED TO ATTEND HER **FUNERAL** THE FOLLOWING MONDAY AT THREE O'CLOCK IN THE AFTERNOON.

I KEPT THINKING OF MY SISTER IN HER CHAIR BY THE FIRE. I WROTE TO JOE TO SAY I WOULD COME TO THE *FUNERAL*.

DEAR JOE, HOW ARE YOU?

PIP, OLD *CHAP*, YOU KNEW HER WHEN SHE WAS YOUNG AND WELL.

Here they come!

Here they are!

WE WENT INTO THE *CHURCHYARD*, AND MY SISTER WAS LAID QUIETLY IN THE EARTH, NEAR OUR PARENTS.

AFTERWARDS, BIDDY, JOE AND I HAD A COLD DINNER TOGETHER IN THE BEST ROOM AT HOME. JOE WAS SO CAREFUL ABOUT HIS TABLE MANNERS THAT WE FELT UNCOMFORTABLE. HE WAS VERY PLEASED WHEN I ASKED IF I COULD SLEEP IN MY OWN LITTLE ROOM.

IN THE EVENING, I HAD A LITTLE TALK WITH BIDDY.

I SUPPOSE IT WILL BE DIFFICULT FOR YOU TO LIVE HERE NOW, BIDDY DEAR?

OH, I CAN'T STAY, MR PIP.

HOW ARE YOU GOING TO LIVE? IF YOU WANT ANY MO—

HOW AM I GOING TO LIVE? I'M GOING TO TRY TO GET THE PLACE OF TEACHER IN THE NEW SCHOOL HERE.

I HAVEN'T HEARD HOW MY SISTER DIED, BIDDY.

SHE HAD BEEN ILL FOR FOUR DAYS WHEN SHE SAID QUITE CLEARLY, 'JOE'.

I RAN AND FETCHED HIM. SHE LAID HER HEAD ON HIS SHOULDER.

SHE SAID 'JOE' AGAIN, 'PARDON' AND 'PIP'. AN HOUR LATER, SHE WAS DEAD.

DO YOU KNOW WHAT'S HAPPENED TO ORLICK? HAVE YOU SEEN HIM?

WHY ARE YOU LOOKING AT THAT DARK TREE?

I SAW HIM THERE ON THE NIGHT SHE DIED, AND I'VE JUST SEEN HIM THERE.

I WAS ANGRY THAT HE WAS STILL FOLLOWING HER. I TOLD HER I WOULD DRIVE HIM AWAY.

BIDDY TOLD ME HOW JOE LOVED ME, AND NEVER COMPLAINED OF ANYTHING, BUT ALWAYS DID HIS DUTY WITH A GENTLE HEART.

BIDDY, WE MUST TALK OF THESE THINGS OFTEN, BECAUSE I WILL BE DOWN HERE OFTEN. I'M NOT GOING TO LEAVE POOR JOE ALONE.

ARE YOU QUITE SURE THAT YOU *WILL* COME TO SEE HIM OFTEN?

REALLY, BIDDY!

PLEASE DON'T SAY ANY MORE.

DURING THE NIGHT I THOUGHT HOW UNFAIR BIDDY HAD BEEN TO ME.

GOODBYE, DEAR JOE! I'LL BE BACK SOON, AND OFTEN.

IT'S NEVER TOO SOON, SIR, AND NEVER TOO OFTEN.

BIDDY, I'M NOT ANGRY, BUT I'M HURT.

DON'T BE HURT. LET ME BE HURT, IF I'VE BEEN UNFAIR.

AGAIN, THE **MISTS** WERE RISING AS I WALKED AWAY FROM THE **FORGE**. BIDDY WAS RIGHT.

I WAS NOT GOING TO COME BACK.

85

HERBERT'S DEBTS AND MINE INCREASED. I HAD MY TWENTY-FIRST BIRTHDAY. I WAS SURE THAT MR JAGGERS WOULD TELL ME SOMETHING THEN.

I RECEIVED A NOTE FROM WEMMICK. IT SAID THAT MR JAGGERS WISHED TO SEE ME AT FIVE IN THE AFTERNOON ON MY BIRTHDAY.

CONGRATULATIONS, MR PIP. TAKE A SEAT.

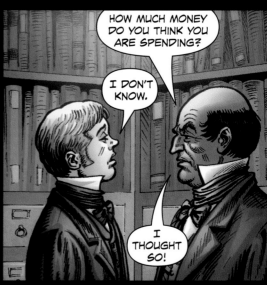

HOW MUCH MONEY DO YOU THINK YOU ARE SPENDING?

I DON'T KNOW.

I THOUGHT SO!

DO YOU HAVE ANYTHING TO ASK ME?

CAN YOU TELL ME WHO MY **BENEFACTOR** IS TODAY?

NO. ASK ME ANOTHER QUESTION.

HAVE YOU GOT SOMETHING TO GIVE ME, SIR?

I THOUGHT YOU'D ASK ME THAT! YOU'VE BEEN TAKING A LOT FROM HERE, BUT YOU'RE IN DEBT, AREN'T YOU?

YES, SIR.

HERE IS FIVE HUNDRED POUNDS. YOU MUST LIVE ON THIS AMOUNT EACH YEAR UNTIL YOUR **BENEFACTOR** APPEARS.

YOU MUST NOW LOOK AFTER YOUR MONEY **AFFAIRS** YOURSELF.

WILL MY BENEFACTOR COME SOON TO LONDON, OR ASK ME TO GO SOMEWHERE ELSE?

YOU MUSTN'T ASK ME THAT. I CAN'T ANSWER.

I REALISED THAT MISS HAVISHAM HAD NOT TOLD HIM HER PLAN FOR ME AND ESTELLA.

IF THAT'S ALL YOU CAN TELL ME, I HAVE NOTHING ELSE TO SAY.

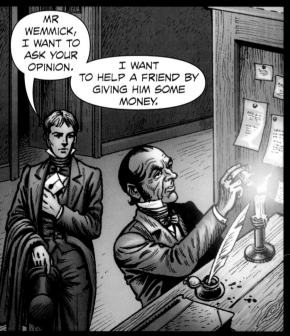

MR WEMMICK, I WANT TO ASK YOUR OPINION.

I WANT TO HELP A FRIEND BY GIVING HIM SOME MONEY.

IT WOULD BE BETTER TO THROW YOUR MONEY INTO THE RIVER.

DON'T DO IT, UNLESS YOU WANT TO LOSE THE FRIEND.

THE NEXT SUNDAY AFTERNOON I WENT TO WEMMICK'S CASTLE.

WEMMICK'S FATHER OPENED THE DOOR AND TOLD ME HIS SON WOULD BE HOME SOON FROM HIS WALK. WE SAT BY THE FIRE. THE OLD MAN TALKED AND I NODDED. SUDDENLY THERE WAS A NOISE IN THE WALL, AND A LITTLE WOODEN **FLAP** OPENED. 'JOHN' WAS WRITTEN ON IT.

Click

MY SON'S COME HOME!

John

WE WENT OUT TO THE BRIDGE AND WEMMICK'S FATHER LOWERED IT. WEMMICK CAME ACROSS AND INTRODUCED ME TO MISS SKIFFINS.

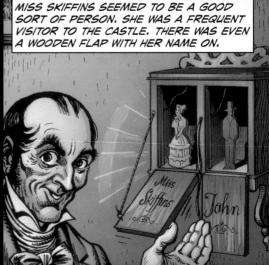

MISS SKIFFINS SEEMED TO BE A GOOD SORT OF PERSON. SHE WAS A FREQUENT VISITOR TO THE CASTLE. THERE WAS EVEN A WOODEN FLAP WITH HER NAME ON.

Miss Skiffins

John

WEMMICK AND I WENT FOR A WALK AROUND THE CASTLE. I TOLD HIM ABOUT HERBERT AND HOW I WAS WORRIED ABOUT HIM.

I THINK I, AND MY **EXPECTATIONS**, HAVE BEEN BAD FOR HIM. HOW CAN I HELP HIM?

THIS IS VERY GOOD OF YOU, MR PIP.

I'LL THINK ABOUT IT. I'LL ASK MISS SKIFFINS'S BROTHER TOO. HE'S AN **ACCOUNTANT** AND AN **AGENT**.

THANK YOU SO MUCH.

A FEW DAYS LATER, I RECEIVED A NOTE FROM WEMMICK. HE HAD FOUND SOMEONE WHO SOLD SHIPS, CALLED CLARRIKER. HE WANTED MONEY AND A PARTNER.

I SIGNED SOME PAPERS AND PAID CLARRIKER HALF OF MY FIVE HUNDRED POUNDS.

I AGREED TO PAY HIM MORE LATER. EVERYTHING WAS SO CLEVERLY MANAGED THAT HERBERT DIDN'T SUSPECT ANYTHING.

I WILL NEVER FORGET HERBERT'S FACE WHEN HE TOLD ME ABOUT HIS JOB WITH CLARRIKER. HE BELIEVED THAT AT LAST HIS CHANCE HAD COME. DAY BY DAY HIS HOPES GREW STRONGER AND HIS FACE GREW BRIGHTER.

I WAS VERY HAPPY.

BOTH IN AND OUT OF MRS BRANDLEY'S HOUSE, ESTELLA CAUSED ME ALL KINDS OF PAIN.

WHEN I DIE, MY GHOST WILL LIVE IN THE HOUSE IN RICHMOND WHERE ESTELLA LIVED. MY TROUBLED **SPIRIT** WAS ALWAYS THERE WHILE SHE WAS THERE.

SHE LIVED WITH A WOMAN CALLED MRS BRANDLEY. SHE HAD BEEN A FRIEND OF MISS HAVISHAM'S WHEN THEY WERE YOUNG.

SHE MADE FUN OF MY LOVE FOR HER, AND USED ME TO HURT HER MANY OTHER ADMIRERS.

I OFTEN VISITED HER AT RICHMOND.

PIP, WILL YOU NEVER LISTEN TO MY WARNING?

OF WHAT? NOT TO BE ATTRACTED TO YOU, DO YOU MEAN?

IF YOU DON'T KNOW WHAT I MEAN, YOU ARE **BLIND.**

MISS HAVISHAM WANTS TO SEE ME FOR A DAY. SHE WANTS YOU TO TAKE ME AND BRING ME BACK. WILL YOU? SHE WANTS US TO GO THE DAY AFTER TOMORROW.

MISS HAVISHAM WAS **FONDER** OF ESTELLA THAN EVER. SHE LOOKED AT HER WITH ADMIRATION.

HOW DOES SHE TREAT YOU, PIP?

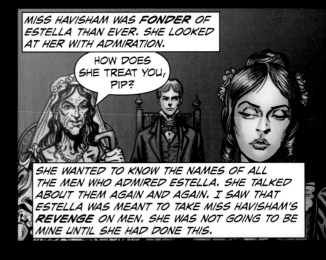

SHE WANTED TO KNOW THE NAMES OF ALL THE MEN WHO ADMIRED ESTELLA. SHE TALKED ABOUT THEM AGAIN AND AGAIN. I SAW THAT ESTELLA WAS MEANT TO TAKE MISS HAVISHAM'S **REVENGE** ON MEN. SHE WAS NOT GOING TO BE MINE UNTIL SHE HAD DONE THIS.

ON THIS VISIT, SOME ANGRY WORDS WERE EXCHANGED BY ESTELLA AND MISS HAVISHAM. IT WAS THE FIRST TIME I HAD SEEN THEM ANGRY WITH EACH OTHER. WE WERE SEATED BY THE FIRE, AND ESTELLA BEGAN TO TAKE HER ARM AWAY FROM MISS HAVISHAM'S.

WHAT! ARE YOU TIRED OF ME?

I'M ONLY A LITTLE TIRED OF MYSELF.

SPEAK THE TRUTH, YOU **UNGRATEFUL** GIRL! YOU'RE TIRED OF ME! YOU'RE COLD, SO COLD!

WHAT? YOU'RE THE ONE WHO'S MADE ME COLD!

SO PROUD! SO HARD! BUT HOW CAN YOU BE PROUD AND HARD TO ME!

YOU TAUGHT ME TO BE PROUD AND HARD. I CAN'T UNDERSTAND WHY YOU'RE BEHAVING LIKE THIS. I'VE NEVER FORGOTTEN WHAT HAPPENED TO YOU. I'VE ALWAYS DONE WHAT YOU TOLD ME TO DO. I HAVE NEVER SHOWN ANY WEAKNESS.

YOU MUST TAKE ME AS YOU HAVE MADE ME.

WHEN I RETURNED, EVERYTHING WAS BACK TO NORMAL. WE PLAYED CARDS, THE EVENING PASSED, AND I WENT TO BED.

THE NEXT DAY THEY DID NOT ARGUE AGAIN, AND THEY NEVER DID ON ANY OTHER VISITS.

IT IS IMPOSSIBLE TO TURN THIS PAGE OF MY LIFE WITHOUT PUTTING BENTLEY DRUMMLE'S NAME UPON IT. ON ONE OCCASION, HE ASKED US TO DRINK TO ...

ESTELLA OF RICHMOND!

I KNOW THAT LADY.

SO DO I.

I SOON LEARNT THAT THEY HAD DANCED TOGETHER SEVERAL TIMES.

I FOUND OUT THAT DRUMMLE HAD BEGUN TO FOLLOW ESTELLA CLOSELY. SHE ALLOWED HIM TO DO IT. SOON HE WAS ALWAYS FOLLOWING HER, AND I SAW HIM EVERY DAY.

AT A DANCE IN RICHMOND, DRUMMLE STAYED CLOSE TO ESTELLA FOR MUCH OF THE EVENING AND SHE ALLOWED HIM TO. I DECIDED TO SPEAK TO HER WHILE SHE WAS WAITING FOR MRS BRANDLEY TO TAKE HER HOME.

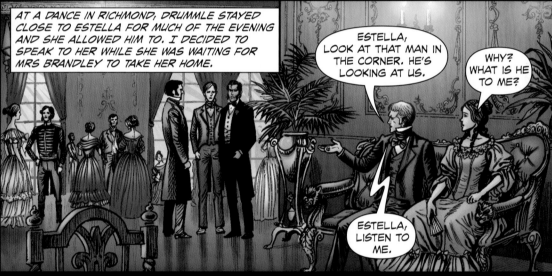

ESTELLA, LOOK AT THAT MAN IN THE CORNER. HE'S LOOKING AT US.

WHY? WHAT IS HE TO ME?

ESTELLA, LISTEN TO ME.

IT MAKES ME **MISERABLE** THAT YOU ARE ENCOURAGING A MAN LIKE DRUMMLE.

DON'T BE FOOLISH, PIP. MY ENCOURAGEMENT MAY HURT OTHERS, AND PERHAPS IT'S MEANT TO. IT'S NOT WORTH DISCUSSING.

ARE YOU GIVING HIM FALSE HOPE, ESTELLA?

YES, AND MANY OTHERS. ALL OF THEM, EXCEPT YOU.

HERE'S MRS BRANDLEY. I'LL SAY NO MORE.

VOLUME II
CHAPTER XX

THE TURNING POINT OF MY LIFE THEN OCCURRED. I WAS TWENTY-THREE, AND I HAD NOT HEARD ANYTHING ABOUT MY *EXPECTATIONS*. WE HAD LEFT BARNARD'S *INN* AND WERE LIVING IN TEMPLE, DOWN BY THE RIVER. MR POCKET WAS NO LONGER MY TEACHER, BUT I READ FOR HOURS EACH DAY.

HERBERT WAS IN MARSEILLE ON BUSINESS, SO I WAS ALONE. IT WAS *AWFUL* WEATHER; STORMY AND WET. AT ELEVEN O'CLOCK ONE NIGHT, WHEN I HAD JUST FINISHED READING, I HEARD A *FOOTSTEP* ON THE STAIRS.

CLUMP

I TOOK MY LAMP AND WENT OUT. WHOEVER WAS BELOW HAD STOPPED. EVERYTHING WAS QUIET.

WHO'S THERE? WHAT FLOOR DO YOU WANT?

THE TOP. MR PIP.

THAT'S MY NAME. IS SOMETHING THE MATTER?

NO.

I DIDN'T RECOGNISE HIM, BUT HE LOOKED PLEASED TO SEE ME.

WHAT DO YOU WANT? WOULD YOU LIKE TO COME IN?

YES, I WOULD. I'LL EXPLAIN MY BUSINESS, *MASTER*.

THERE'S NO ONE HERE, IS THERE?

WHY DO YOU ASK?

DON'T TAKE HOLD OF ME.

YOU'D BE SORRY AFTERWARDS IF YOU DID.

I DECIDED NOT TO TAKE HOLD OF HIM BECAUSE ...

... I RECOGNISED HIM!

HE WAS MY PRISONER. THERE WAS NO NEED FOR HIM TO SHOW ME THE FILE.

YOU WERE GOOD TO ME, MY BOY! I'VE NEVER FORGOTTEN IT!

STAY AWAY!

IF YOU ARE GRATEFUL TO ME, I HOPE YOU HAVE SHOWN THIS BY CHANGING YOUR WAY OF LIFE. IT ISN'T NECESSARY TO THANK ME. YOU MUST UNDERSTAND – I –

WHAT MUST I UNDERSTAND?

THAT I CAN'T HAVE ANY CONTACT WITH YOU NOW. I'M PLEASED THAT YOU HAVE COME TO THANK ME, BUT OUR LIVES ARE VERY DIFFERENT.

I MADE HIM A DRINK. WHEN I GAVE IT TO HIM, I SAW THAT HIS EYES WERE FULL OF TEARS.

I'M SORRY IF I SPOKE UNKINDLY TO YOU. I HOPE YOU ARE WELL AND HAPPY!

I'VE BEEN A SHEEP FARMER IN THE NEW WORLD, THOUSANDS OF MILES AWAY FROM HERE.

I HOPE YOU'VE DONE WELL?

I'VE DONE WONDERFULLY WELL. NO ONE HAS DONE AS WELL AS ME. I'M FAMOUS FOR IT.

I'M PLEASED TO HEAR IT.

HAVE YOU EVER SEEN THE MAN YOU SENT TO ME? HE BROUGHT ME TWO ONE-POUND NOTES.

TO A POOR BOY, THEY WERE A SMALL *FORTUNE*. BUT, LIKE YOU, I HAVE DONE WELL SINCE, AND YOU MUST LET ME PAY THEM BACK.

HOW HAVE YOU DONE WELL SINCE YOU AND I WERE OUT ON THOSE COLD *MARSHES*?

I BEGAN TO SHAKE A LITTLE. I TOLD HIM THAT I HAD BEEN CHOSEN TO *INHERIT* SOME PROPERTY.

I FELT FULL OF HATRED FOR HIM.

I'M YOUR SECOND FATHER. I'VE SAVED MONEY, ONLY FOR YOU TO SPEND.

WHEN I WAS LIVING ALONE, AND WAS LOOKING AFTER SHEEP, I USED TO SEE YOUR FACE, MANY TIMES.

I SAID, 'IF I GET FREEDOM AND MONEY, I'LL MAKE THAT BOY A **GENTLEMAN**!' AND I DID IT. YOUR HOUSE AND CLOTHES COULDN'T BE BETTER! AND YOU'VE GOT SO MANY BOOKS!

DIDN'T YOU EVER THINK IT MIGHT BE ME THAT HAD GIVEN YOU THE MONEY?

OH NO, NO. NEVER, NEVER!

WAS THERE NO ONE ELSE?

NO. WHO ELSE WOULD THERE BE? EVERYTHING I'VE DONE HAS BEEN FOR YOU.

IT WASN'T EASY FOR ME TO COME ALL THE WAY HERE, NOR WAS IT SAFE. BUT I'VE DONE IT AT LAST!

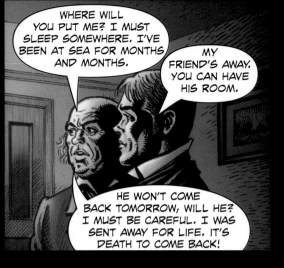

WHERE WILL YOU PUT ME? I MUST SLEEP SOMEWHERE. I'VE BEEN AT SEA FOR MONTHS AND MONTHS.

MY FRIEND'S AWAY. YOU CAN HAVE HIS ROOM.

HE WON'T COME BACK TOMORROW, WILL HE? I MUST BE CAREFUL. I WAS SENT AWAY FOR LIFE. IT'S DEATH TO COME BACK!

HE WENT TO BED IN HERBERT'S ROOM. I SAT DOWN BY THE FIRE. I WAS TOO AFRAID TO GO TO BED. I REALISED HOW EVERYTHING HAD FALLEN TO PIECES.

MISS HAVISHAM'S PLANS FOR ME WERE JUST A DREAM.

ESTELLA WAS NOT MEANT FOR ME.

THE SHARPEST AND DEEPEST PAIN CAME FROM REALISING THAT I HAD LEFT JOE FOR THIS *PRISONER*.

WHEN I WOKE UP AT FIVE, THE FIRE AND CANDLES HAD GONE OUT. THERE WAS ONLY DARKNESS, WIND AND RAIN.

I HAD TO ENSURE THE SAFETY OF MY VISITOR SO I DECIDED TO TELL PEOPLE THAT MY **UNCLE** HAD UNEXPECTEDLY COME FROM THE COUNTRY.

WHAT ARE YOU DOING THERE?

I ASKED THE **WATCHMAN** WHETHER HE HAD LET ANY STRANGERS IN AT THE GATE.

A STRANGER ASKED FOR YOU AT ABOUT ELEVEN O'CLOCK.

MY UNCLE, YES.

DID YOU SEE HIM, SIR? AND THE PERSON WITH HIM?

PERSON WITH HIM?

I THOUGHT THEY WERE TOGETHER. THEY BOTH WENT THE SAME WAY.

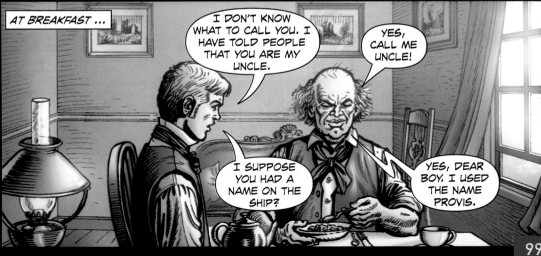

AT BREAKFAST ...

I DON'T KNOW WHAT TO CALL YOU. I HAVE TOLD PEOPLE THAT YOU ARE MY UNCLE.

YES, CALL ME UNCLE!

I SUPPOSE YOU HAD A NAME ON THE SHIP?

YES, DEAR BOY. I USED THE NAME PROVIS.

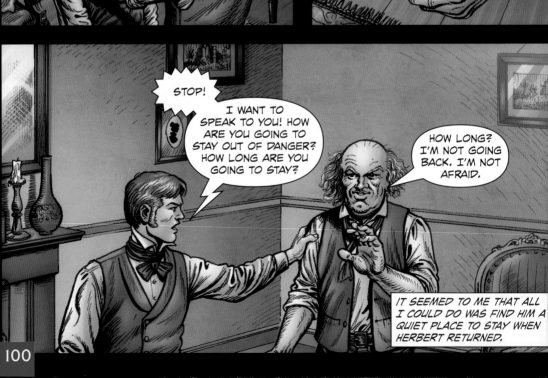

PIP, BE CAREFUL. DON'T TELL ME ANYTHING. I DON'T WANT TO KNOW.

HE KNOWS MAGWITCH HAS COME.

MR JAGGERS, I WANT TO KNOW IF HE HAS TOLD ME THE TRUTH.

DID YOU SAY 'TOLD' OR 'INFORMED'?

'TOLD' MEANS HE HAS SPOKEN TO YOU. HE CAN'T DO THAT IN NEW SOUTH WALES.

ABEL MAGWITCH HAS INFORMED ME THAT HE IS MY **BENEFACTOR**.

THAT'S HIM. IN NEW SOUTH WALES.

AND ONLY HE IS MY BENEFACTOR?

ONLY HE.

I DON'T THINK YOU ARE RESPONSIBLE FOR MY MISTAKE, BUT I ALWAYS THOUGHT MISS HAVISHAM WAS MY BENEFACTOR.

AS YOU SAY, PIP, I AM NOT RESPONSIBLE FOR THAT.

WHEN MAGWITCH WROTE TO ME HE SEEMED TO SAY THAT HE WANTED TO SEE YOU IN ENGLAND. I SAID I MUST HEAR NO MORE OF THAT. IT WOULD BE AGAINST THE LAW, AND HE COULD DIE.

SOMEONE CALLED PROVIS WROTE AND ASKED FOR YOUR ADDRESS. HE WANTED IT FOR MAGWITCH.

WE SHOOK HANDS AND SAID GOODBYE.

I HATED HIM MORE AND MORE, AS HE BECAME **FONDER** OF ME. FOR FIVE DAYS I DID NOT DARE GO OUT WITH HIM, EXCEPT AT NIGHT.

101

ONE EVENING, I WAS WOKEN BY *FOOTSTEPS* ON THE STAIRS.

QUIET!

IT'S HERBERT!

HANDEL, HOW ARE YOU? YOU'VE GROWN THIN AND *PALE*!

HANDEL, MY —

HELLO!

HERBERT, THIS IS A VISITOR OF MINE.

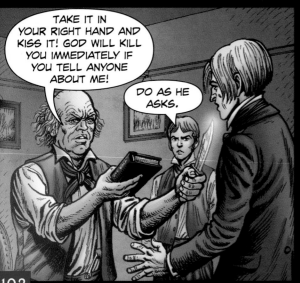

TAKE IT IN YOUR RIGHT HAND AND KISS IT! GOD WILL KILL YOU IMMEDIATELY IF YOU TELL ANYONE ABOUT ME!

DO AS HE ASKS.

NOW YOU'VE PROMISED TO GOD THAT YOU WON'T SAY ANYTHING.

HERBERT, PROVIS AND I SAT DOWN BY THE FIRE AND I TOLD HIM THE SECRET. I SAW THAT HE WAS AS SHOCKED AS I WAS.

AT MIDNIGHT I TOOK PROVIS TO HIS ROOMS. WHEN HIS DOOR CLOSED, I FELT SAFE FOR THE FIRST TIME SINCE HE HAD ARRIVED.

SOMETHING MUST BE DONE. HE WANTS TO SPEND MONEY ON ALL KINDS OF EXPENSIVE THINGS. HE MUST BE STOPPED SOMEHOW.

YOU MEAN THAT YOU CAN'T ACCEPT —

HOW CAN I? LOOK AT HIM! THE **AWFUL** THING IS THAT HE'S VERY **FOND** OF ME.

BUT EVEN IF I NEVER TAKE ANOTHER PENNY FROM HIM, THINK OF WHAT I **OWE** HIM ALREADY! AND I HAVE LARGE DEBTS, AND I NOW HAVE NO **EXPECTATIONS**.

I AM NOT FIT TO WORK ANYWHERE!

WE HAVE TO GET HIM OUT OF ENGLAND. YOU'LL HAVE TO GO WITH HIM, AND THEN YOU CAN LEAVE HIM.

WE'LL DO IT TOGETHER.

THE NEXT MORNING, HE CAME ROUND AND HAD BREAKFAST. THEN HE TOLD US HIS STORY ...

THE SHORT STORY OF MY LIFE IS IN **PRISON** AND OUT OF PRISON, IN PRISON AND OUT OF PRISON.

I'VE HAD EVERY PUNISHMENT YOU CAN THINK OF.

I DON'T KNOW WHERE I WAS BORN. AS A CHILD, I WALKED AROUND THE COUNTRY, ASKED FOR MONEY, STOLE AND WORKED WHEN I COULD.

MORE THAN TWENTY YEARS AGO I MET A MAN WHO I'D LIKE TO HIT WITH THIS **POKER**. HIS NAME WAS COMPEYSON. THAT'S THE MAN YOU SAW ON THE **MARSHES**.

I BEGAN TO WORK FOR COMPEYSON. HE'D BEEN TO SCHOOL AND PRETENDED TO BE A **GENTLEMAN**. HE MADE MONEY BY CHEATING PEOPLE OUT OF THEIR MONEY.

HE WORKED WITH ANOTHER MAN CALLED ARTHUR.

SOME YEARS BEFORE, THEY HAD CHEATED A RICH LADY OUT OF A LOT OF MONEY BUT HAD SPENT IT ALL.

ARTHUR WAS DYING, AND COMPEYSON'S WIFE WAS LOOKING AFTER HIM WHEN SHE COULD.

I WON'T TELL YOU ALL THE DETAILS, BUT COMPEYSON GOT ME IN DEBT TO HIM.

HE WAS YOUNGER THAN ME, BUT HE WAS MUCH CLEVERER.

I WENT TO THE OLD HOUSE AND FOUND MISS HAVISHAM AND ESTELLA.

WHAT BRINGS YOU HERE, PIP?

I CAME TO SPEAK TO ESTELLA.

I WILL SAY WHAT I WANTED TO SAY TO ESTELLA IN A MOMENT. IT WILL PLEASE YOU TO KNOW THAT I'M AS UNHAPPY AS YOU MEANT ME TO BE.

I HAVE FOUND OUT WHO MY **BENEFACTOR** IS, AND IT'S NOT A PLEASANT DISCOVERY. IT WILL NOT HELP ME IN ANY WAY. I CAN'T TELL YOU MORE THAN THAT.

WHEN YOU FIRST BROUGHT ME HERE, MISS HAVISHAM, I SUPPOSE I WAS LIKE A SERVANT? AND MR JAGGERS –

MR JAGGERS HAD NOTHING TO DO WITH IT. IT'S JUST CHANCE THAT HE IS MY LAWYER AND YOUR BENEFACTOR'S LAWYER.

YOU KNEW THAT I THOUGHT YOU WERE MY BENEFACTOR, AND YOU SAID NOTHING TO ME. YOU WANTED TO PUNISH YOUR RELATIONS.

I DID. BUT YOU HAVE CAUSED THIS TROUBLE YOURSELF.

I KNOW SOME OF YOUR RELATIONS. YOU ARE VERY WRONG IF YOU THINK THAT MR MATTHEW POCKET AND HIS SON HERBERT ARE NOT HONEST AND KIND.

WHAT DO YOU WANT FOR THEM?

ONLY THAT YOU DON'T THINK THEY ARE THE SAME AS THE OTHERS.

I CANNOT HIDE FROM YOU THAT THERE IS SOMETHING THAT I WANT. COULD YOU GIVE SOME MONEY TO HERBERT?

I BEGAN HELPING HIM TWO YEARS AGO, WITHOUT HIS KNOWLEDGE, BUT I CAN'T CONTINUE TO DO SO NOW. I CAN'T EXPLAIN WHY.

WHAT ELSE?

ESTELLA, YOU KNOW I LOVE YOU, AND HAVE LOVED YOU FOR A LONG TIME.

I KNOW THAT YOU WILL NEVER BE MINE, ESTELLA, BUT I STILL LOVE YOU. I HAVE LOVED YOU SINCE I FIRST SAW YOU IN THIS HOUSE.

IT WAS UNKIND OF MISS HAVISHAM TO MAKE ME LOVE YOU. I THINK THAT IN HER OWN PAIN, SHE FORGOT MINE.

WHEN YOU SAY YOU LOVE ME, I UNDERSTAND THE WORDS, BUT THAT'S ALL.

I'VE TRIED TO WARN YOU OF THIS, HAVEN'T I?

I HOPED YOU DIDN'T MEAN IT. YOU'RE SO YOUNG AND BEAUTIFUL! IT'S UNNATURAL!

IT'S NATURAL FOR ME – IT'S THE WAY I WAS MADE. I ONLY TELL THIS TO YOU – NO OTHERS. I CAN'T DO ANY MORE.

ISN'T IT TRUE THAT BENTLEY DRUMMLE IS HERE?

AND THAT YOU RIDE OUT WITH HIM? YOU CAN'T LOVE HIM! YOU WOULDN'T MARRY HIM, ESTELLA?

WHY NOT TELL YOU THE TRUTH? YES, I'M GOING TO MARRY HIM.

DEAREST ESTELLA, DON'T LET MISS HAVISHAM LEAD YOU INTO THIS.

YOU SHOULD MARRY SOMEONE MUCH BETTER THAN DRUMMLE! MISS HAVISHAM GIVES YOU TO HIM TO HURT ALL THE BETTER MEN WHO LOVE AND ADMIRE YOU.

THIS IS MY DECISION, NOT MISS HAVISHAM'S. SHE WANTED ME TO WAIT, BUT I'M TIRED OF THE LIFE I'VE LED.

OH, ESTELLA! HOW CAN I BE HAPPY WHEN YOU ARE DRUMMLE'S WIFE?!?

THIS IS SILLY. YOU'LL FORGET ABOUT ME IN A WEEK.

FORGET YOU!

YOU HAVE BEEN PART OF ME SINCE I FIRST CAME HERE.

YOU WILL BE PART OF ME UNTIL THE LAST HOUR OF MY LIFE.

I PRAY THAT GOD FORGIVES YOU!

I LEFT THE HOUSE AND BEGAN TO WALK TO LONDON. I COULDN'T BEAR TO GO BACK TO THE BLUE BOAR AND SEE DRUMMLE. THE BEST THING I COULD DO WAS TO COMPLETELY TIRE MYSELF.

IT WAS AFTER MIDNIGHT WHEN I ARRIVED AT WHITEFRIARS GATE. THE WATCHMAN EXAMINED ME CLOSELY.

I THOUGHT IT WAS YOU, SIR. HERE'S A NOTE. THE MAN WHO BROUGHT IT ASKED YOU TO READ IT BY MY LAMP.

I TOOK THE NOTE. ON THE TOP WERE THE WORDS, 'PLEASE READ THIS HERE'. I OPENED IT AND READ, IN WEMMICK'S WRITING:

Don't go home.

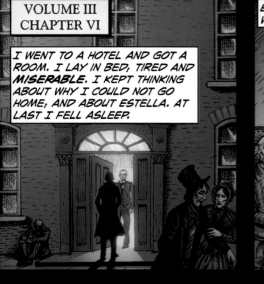

I WENT TO A HOTEL AND GOT A ROOM. I LAY IN BED, TIRED AND **MISERABLE**. I KEPT THINKING ABOUT WHY I COULD NOT GO HOME, AND ABOUT ESTELLA. AT LAST I FELL ASLEEP.

EARLY THE NEXT MORNING I WENT TO SEE WEMMICK.

HELLO, MR PIP! WOULD YOU MIND COOKING THIS FOR MY FATHER?

NOT AT ALL. I'D BE HAPPY TO.

YESTERDAY MORNING, I HEARD, BY ACCIDENT, NEWS OF SOMEONE. HE LIVES IN A PART OF THE WORLD WHERE MANY PEOPLE ARE SENT. HE'S DISAPPEARED AND PEOPLE ARE TALKING ABOUT HIM.

I ALSO HEARD THAT SOMEONE'S BEEN WATCHING YOU IN YOUR ROOMS.

I TOLD HIM THAT I WOULD LIKE TO ASK HIM A QUESTION, BUT THAT HE DIDN'T HAVE TO ANSWER. HE NODDED.

HAVE YOU HEARD OF A MAN CALLED COMPEYSON? IS HE ALIVE? IS HE IN LONDON?

WEMMICK NODDED TO ALL THESE QUESTIONS.

I WENT TO YOUR ROOMS TO FIND YOU. THEN I WENT TO CLARRIKER'S TO FIND MR HERBERT.

I TOLD HIM THAT IF THERE WAS ANYONE IN THE ROOMS OR NEARBY, HE SHOULD MOVE HIM SOMEWHERE ELSE, BUT NOT SOMEWHERE TOO FAR AWAY.

MR HERBERT SUGGESTED THAT THE MAN MOVE TO THE HOUSE WHERE HIS YOUNG LADY AND HER FATHER LIVE.

IT'S NEAR THE RIVER AND THERE ARE SOME EMPTY ROOMS ON THE TOP FLOOR THAT HE COULD RENT. I THOUGHT IT WAS A VERY GOOD IDEA.

LATER, IF YOU WANTED TO PUT HIM ON A SHIP, IT WOULD BE EASY.

WELL! MR HERBERT MOVED THE MAN LAST NIGHT. HERE'S THE ADDRESS. IT'S AT MILL POND BANK.

THANK YOU FOR ALL YOUR HELP.

YOU'RE VERY WELCOME. I MUST GO.

IF YOU HAVE NOTHING YOU NEED TO DO, STAY HERE TILL IT'S DARK.

I SOON FELL ASLEEP BY WEMMICK'S FIRE. WHEN IT WAS DARK, I LEFT.

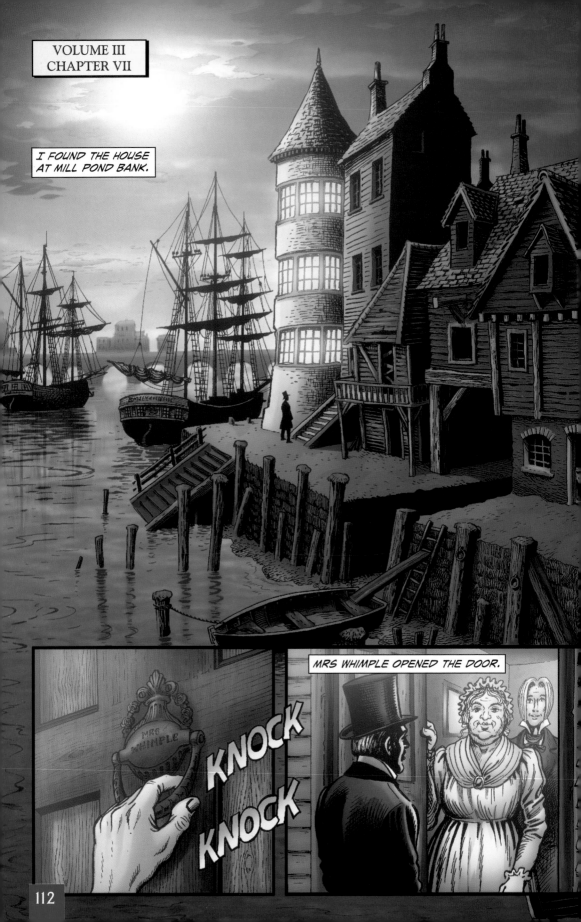

VOLUME III
CHAPTER VII

I FOUND THE HOUSE AT MILL POND BANK.

KNOCK KNOCK

MRS WHIMPLE OPENED THE DOOR.

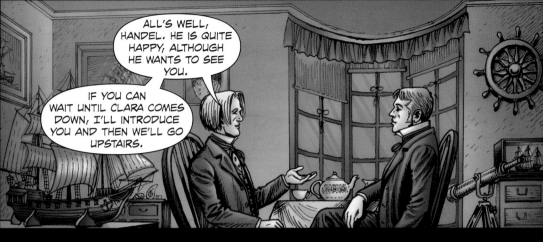

ALL'S WELL, HANDEL. HE IS QUITE HAPPY, ALTHOUGH HE WANTS TO SEE YOU.

IF YOU CAN WAIT UNTIL CLARA COMES DOWN, I'LL INTRODUCE YOU AND THEN WE'LL GO UPSTAIRS.

BANG BANG

BANG BANG

THAT'S HER FATHER. MRS WHIMPLE IS GOOD WITH HIM. I DON'T KNOW WHAT CLARA WOULD DO WITHOUT HER HELP. HER FATHER'S HER ONLY RELATION.

WHAT'S HIS NAME?

MR BARLEY.

THE DOOR OPENED, AND A VERY PRETTY GIRL CAME IN. IT WAS CLARA.

THERE WAS SOMETHING VERY NATURAL, LOVING AND GENTLE ABOUT HER.

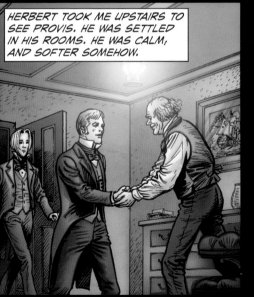

HERBERT TOOK ME UPSTAIRS TO SEE PROVIS. HE WAS SETTLED IN HIS ROOMS. HE WAS CALM, AND SOFTER SOMEHOW.

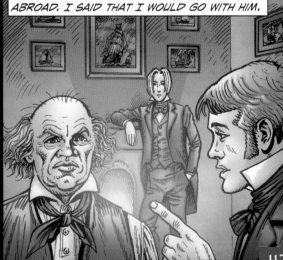

I TOLD HIM WHAT WEMMICK HAD HEARD AND WHAT WEMMICK HAD SAID ABOUT GETTING HIM ABROAD. I SAID THAT I WOULD GO WITH HIM.

113

WE COULD TAKE HIM DOWN THE RIVER OURSELVES, HANDEL.

IF YOU BEGAN TO KEEP A BOAT AT OUR ROOMS, WE COULD REGULARLY GO ROWING IN IT. THEN NO ONE WOULD NOTICE US WHEN WE TOOK HIM OUT.

PROVIS AND I LIKED THIS IDEA. WE DECIDED THAT PROVIS SHOULD WATCH FOR US ON THE RIVER. HE SHOULD PULL DOWN THE **BLIND** ON HIS WINDOW WHENEVER HE SAW US AND EVERYTHING WAS FINE.

I GOT UP TO LEAVE.

I DON'T LIKE TO LEAVE YOU HERE, BUT IT'S SAFER. GOODBYE!

DEAR BOY, I DON'T KNOW WHEN WE MAY MEET AGAIN, BUT I DON'T LIKE GOODBYE. SAY GOODNIGHT!

GOODNIGHT! HERBERT WILL COME AND TELL ME ABOUT YOU. AND WHEN THE TIME COMES, I SHALL BE READY.

NEXT DAY I GOT A BOAT AND BROUGHT IT CLOSE TO MY ROOMS. I BEGAN GOING OUT IN IT, SOMETIMES ALONE AND SOMETIMES WITH HERBERT.

THE FIRST TIME WE PASSED MILL POND BANK, THE BLIND CAME DOWN. HOWEVER, I FELT SOMEONE WAS WATCHING US, AND THIS FEELING STAYED WITH ME.

VOLUME III CHAPTER VIII

SOME WEEKS PASSED.

WE WAITED TO HEAR FROM WEMMICK, BUT HE SAID NOTHING. I NEEDED MONEY, SO I SOLD SOME OF MY *JEWELLERY*.

PLEDGE TOKENS

5/-

I HAD A FEELING THAT ESTELLA WAS MARRIED.

I DIDN'T WANT TO KNOW FOR CERTAIN, SO I DIDN'T LOOK IN THE NEWSPAPERS. I WAS UNHAPPY AND ANXIOUS.

I ROWED IN MY BOAT AND WAITED, WAITED, WAITED.

ON A COLD FEBRUARY EVENING, I WENT TO SEE MR WOPSLE IN A PLAY.

YOU WON'T BELIEVE THIS!

DO YOU REMEMBER ONE CHRISTMAS WHEN WE CHASED AFTER TWO *PRISONERS* WHO'D ESCAPED?

YES.

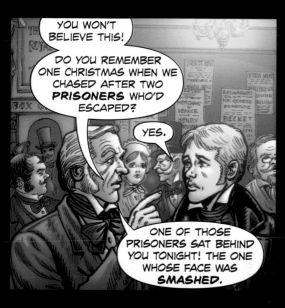

ONE OF THOSE PRISONERS SAT BEHIND YOU TONIGHT! THE ONE WHOSE FACE WAS *SMASHED*.

I FELT TERRIFIED. COMPEYSON HAD BEEN SITTING BEHIND ME!

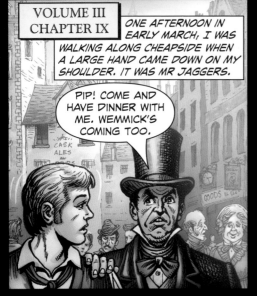

VOLUME III
CHAPTER IX

ONE AFTERNOON IN EARLY MARCH, I WAS WALKING ALONG CHEAPSIDE WHEN A LARGE HAND CAME DOWN ON MY SHOULDER. IT WAS MR JAGGERS.

PIP! COME AND HAVE DINNER WITH ME. WEMMICK'S COMING TOO.

MISS HAVISHAM WANTS TO SEE YOU ON A MATTER OF BUSINESS. WHEN CAN YOU GO?

IF MR PIP INTENDS TO GO IMMEDIATELY, HE NEEDN'T WRITE TO TELL HER.

I UNDERSTOOD FROM THIS THAT I SHOULD GO IMMEDIATELY. I SAID THAT I WOULD GO THE NEXT DAY.

SO, PIP! OUR FRIEND BENTLEY DRUMMLE HAS WON THE LADY!

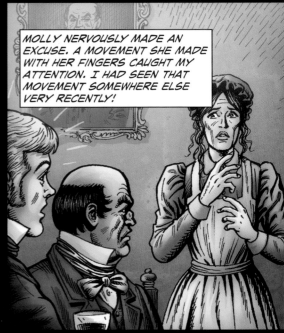

HERE'S TO MRS BENTLEY DRUMMLE!

MOLLY, MOLLY, HOW SLOW YOU ARE TODAY!

MOLLY NERVOUSLY MADE AN EXCUSE. A MOVEMENT SHE MADE WITH HER FINGERS CAUGHT MY ATTENTION. I HAD SEEN THAT MOVEMENT SOMEWHERE ELSE VERY RECENTLY!

I REALISED THAT HER HANDS, EYES AND HAIR WERE ALL FAMILIAR TO ME.

I WAS ABSOLUTELY CERTAIN THAT SHE WAS ESTELLA'S MOTHER.

WEMMICK AND I LEFT TOGETHER.

WEMMICK, YOU ONCE SAID THAT MR JAGGERS'S **HOUSEKEEPER** WAS A WILD ANIMAL THAT HE HAD **TAMED.**

HOW DID HE TAME HER?

THAT'S HIS SECRET. SHE'S BEEN WITH HIM A VERY LONG TIME.

I WISH YOU COULD TELL ME ABOUT HER.

I DON'T KNOW MUCH ABOUT HER.

SHE WAS **TRIED** FOR MURDER, BUT SHE WAS FOUND **INNOCENT.** MR JAGGERS WAS HER LAWYER.

THE MURDERED PERSON WAS A WOMAN WHO WAS OLDER AND MUCH STRONGER.

THE HOUSEKEEPER WAS THE ONLY PERSON WHO WAS SUSPECTED OF THE MURDER.

HOWEVER, AT HER **TRIAL** MR JAGGERS SAID THAT SHE WASN'T STRONG ENOUGH TO KILL THE OTHER WOMAN.

SHE DRESSED VERY CLEVERLY AT HER TRIAL SO SHE LOOKED SMALLER THAN SHE REALLY WAS.

THE OTHER LAWYER TRIED TO PROVE THAT THE TWO WOMEN HAD BEEN FIGHTING OVER A MAN. HE SAID THAT SHE HAD KILLED HER CHILD TO GET HER **REVENGE** ON HIM.

BUT MR JAGGERS SHOWED THAT THE OTHER LAWYER COULD NOT PROVE SHE HAD MURDERED THE WOMAN.

SHE WAS FOUND INNOCENT, AND WENT TO LIVE WITH MR JAGGERS. SHE WAS TAMED THEN.

DO YOU REMEMBER THE SEX OF THE CHILD?

IT WAS A GIRL.

WE SAID GOODNIGHT, AND I WENT HOME WITH SOMETHING NEW TO THINK ABOUT.

I REACHED SATIS HOUSE THE NEXT DAY. I FOUND MISS HAVISHAM IN THE ROOM WITH THE GREAT TABLE. SHE WAS SITTING BY THE FIRE. I FELT SHE WAS EXTREMELY LONELY.

IT'S ME, PIP. MR JAGGERS GAVE ME YOUR NOTE, SO I CAME IMMEDIATELY.

THANK YOU. I WANTED TO TALK TO YOU ABOUT HELPING YOUR FRIEND.

I WANT TO SHOW YOU THAT I AM NOT ALL STONE.

I EXPLAINED WHAT I HAD DONE FOR HERBERT AND HOW I COULD NO LONGER HELP HIM.

IF I GIVE YOU MONEY FOR THIS, WILL YOU KEEP IT A SECRET? HOW MUCH MONEY DO YOU NEED?

NINE HUNDRED POUNDS.

THIS ORDERS MR JAGGERS TO PAY YOU THE MONEY FOR YOUR FRIEND.

IS THERE NOTHING I CAN DO FOR YOU YOURSELF?

THANK YOU FOR ASKING, BUT THERE'S NOTHING.

MY NAME IS ON THERE. IF YOU CAN EVER WRITE UNDER IT, 'I **FORGIVE** HER', PLEASE DO IT!

OH, MISS HAVISHAM, I CAN DO IT NOW.

I WANT FORGIVENESS MYSELF TOO MUCH TO BE ANGRY WITH YOU.

SHE DROPPED ON HER KNEES AT MY FEET. I WAS TERRIBLY SHOCKED. I TRIED TO MAKE HER GET UP, BUT SHE PRESSED MY HAND AND CRIED.

BUT AS SHE GREW AND BECAME MORE BEAUTIFUL, I DID MORE. I STOLE HER HEART, AND PUT ICE IN ITS PLACE.

WHAT HAVE I DONE?!

UNTIL YOU SPOKE ABOUT WHAT YOU FELT, I DIDN'T KNOW WHAT I HAD DONE!

IF YOU CAN MAKE HER BETTER IN ANY SMALL WAY, IT WOULD BE BETTER THAN LIVING IN REGRET.

CAN I ASK YOU SOMETHING ABOUT ESTELLA?

GO ON.

WHOSE CHILD WAS SHE?

BELIEVE ME: WHEN SHE FIRST CAME HERE, I ONLY WANTED TO SAVE HER FROM UNHAPPINESS LIKE MY OWN.

I DON'T KNOW. I TOLD MR JAGGERS THAT I WANTED TO **ADOPT** A LITTLE GIRL. ONE NIGHT HE BROUGHT ESTELLA. SHE WAS TWO OR THREE.

SHE ONLY KNOWS THAT HER PARENTS DIED AND THAT I ADOPTED HER.

I LEFT AND WENT DOWNSTAIRS. I DECIDED TO WALK ROUND THE OLD PLACE AS I FELT I WOULD NEVER BE THERE AGAIN. I WENT ROUND THE GARDEN AND INTO THE **BREWERY**.

I THOUGHT I SAW MISS HAVISHAM. SHE WAS HANGING FROM THE *CEILING*. I SHOOK WITH FEAR ...

... THEN I REALISED SHE WAS NOT REAL.

I WAS SO TERRIFIED THAT I RAN UPSTAIRS. I WANTED TO SEE THAT MISS HAVISHAM WAS SAFE. SHE WAS SITTING CLOSE TO THE FIRE.

AAAARRRRRRGGGGGGHHHHH!!!!

120

I PUSHED HER TO THE FLOOR AND THREW MY COAT OVER HER.

I ALSO USED THE OLD TABLECLOTH.

CLANK!

CHINK!

I DIDN'T KNOW WHAT WAS HAPPENING UNTIL I REALISED WE WERE ON THE FLOOR BY THE GREAT TABLE. THE FIRE WAS OUT, AND SHE LAY STILL. I SENT FOR HELP, AND HELD HER UNTIL IT CAME.

WHEN THE DOCTOR CAME, I WAS SURPRISED TO SEE THAT MY HANDS WERE BURNT. I COULDN'T FEEL THE BURNS.

THE DOCTOR SAID MISS HAVISHAM WAS BADLY HURT, BUT THE MAIN DANGER WAS THE SHOCK.

I DECIDED TO LEAVE EARLY THE NEXT MORNING. BEFORE I LEFT, I KISSED HER, JUST AS SHE SAID ...

Write under my name, "I forgive her."

IS ALL WELL DOWN THE RIVER?

YES. I SAT WITH PROVIS LAST NIGHT FOR TWO HOURS. HE TOLD ME ABOUT A YOUNG WOMAN HE HAD HAD TROUBLE WITH.

SHE WAS ANGRY WITH HIM AND TOOK **REVENGE** IN A TERRIBLE WAY.

WHAT DID SHE DO?

MURDER.

BACK IN OUR ROOMS, HERBERT TOOK CARE OF ME. HE WAS THE KINDEST OF NURSES.

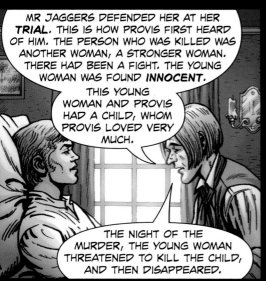

MR JAGGERS DEFENDED HER AT HER **TRIAL**. THIS IS HOW PROVIS FIRST HEARD OF HIM. THE PERSON WHO WAS KILLED WAS ANOTHER WOMAN, A STRONGER WOMAN. THERE HAD BEEN A FIGHT. THE YOUNG WOMAN WAS FOUND **INNOCENT**.

THIS YOUNG WOMAN AND PROVIS HAD A CHILD, WHOM PROVIS LOVED VERY MUCH.

THE NIGHT OF THE MURDER, THE YOUNG WOMAN THREATENED TO KILL THE CHILD, AND THEN DISAPPEARED.

DID SHE KILL THE CHILD?

HE THINKS THAT SHE DID.

HE HID HIMSELF DURING THE TRIAL BECAUSE HE DIDN'T WANT TO SAY ANYTHING THAT COULD LEAD TO HER DEATH.

AFTER THE TRIAL, SHE DISAPPEARED.

DID HE TELL YOU WHEN THIS HAPPENED?

ABOUT THREE OR FOUR YEARS BEFORE HE MET YOU. YOU REMINDED HIM OF THE LITTLE GIRL HE HAD LOST.

HERBERT, THE MAN WE ARE HIDING ...

... IS ESTELLA'S FATHER!

123

THE NEXT MORNING I WENT TO SEE MR JAGGERS.

I TOLD HIM ABOUT MISS HAVISHAM'S ORDER TO GIVE NINE HUNDRED POUNDS TO HERBERT. WEMMICK WROTE THE **CHEQUE.**

I'M SORRY THAT THERE'S NOTHING FOR YOU, PIP.

MISS HAVISHAM ASKED IF SHE COULD HELP ME, AND I SAID NO. I ASKED HER FOR INFORMATION ABOUT HER **ADOPTED** DAUGHTER, AND SHE GAVE ME ALL SHE HAD.

I KNOW MORE ABOUT THE CHILD THAN MISS HAVISHAM DOES. I KNOW HER MOTHER.

MOTHER?

I HAVE SEEN HER IN THE LAST THREE DAYS, AND SO HAVE YOU.

I KNOW HER FATHER TOO.

IT WAS CLEAR THAT MR JAGGERS DID NOT KNOW WHO HER FATHER WAS.

YOU KNOW THE YOUNG LADY'S FATHER, PIP?

YES. HIS NAME IS PROVIS – FROM NEW SOUTH WALES.

MR JAGGERS LOOKED SHOCKED.

WHY DOES PROVIS SAY HE IS HER FATHER?

HE DOES NOT SAY SO. HE THINKS SHE IS DEAD.

**VOLUME III
CHAPTER XIII**

I WENT, WITH MY **CHEQUE** IN MY POCKET, TO MISS SKIFFINS'S BROTHER, AND WE WENT TO CLARRIKER.

HE TOLD US THAT BUSINESS WAS GOING WELL. HE WAS GOING TO OPEN A BRANCH IN THE EAST AND HERBERT WAS GOING TO MANAGE IT.

I WAS SAD TO LOSE HERBERT, BUT HE WAS VERY HAPPY AND I TOOK PLEASURE IN THAT. EVERY NIGHT HE CAME HOME AND TOLD ME OF HIS PLANS FOR HIMSELF AND CLARA. MY LEFT ARM WAS TAKING A LONG TIME TO GET BETTER, BUT I COULD USE MY RIGHT ARM QUITE WELL.

ONE MONDAY MORNING I RECEIVED A LETTER FROM WEMMICK.

> Burn this when you have read it. On Wednesday you could do what you have planned, if you want to.

HERBERT AND I CONSIDERED WHAT TO DO. WE COULDN'T HIDE EASILY NOW BECAUSE OF MY INJURED ARMS.

I THINK WE SHOULD TAKE STARTOP. HE'S VERY GOOD WITH BOATS AND HE LIKES US. WE DON'T NEED TO TELL HIM MUCH.

AS FOREIGN SHIPS LEFT LONDON AT HIGH-WATER, OUR PLAN WAS TO GO DOWN THE RIVER AT LOW-WATER AND WAIT IN A QUIET PLACE UNTIL WE COULD GET ONTO A SHIP.

WE DECIDED THAT ONE THAT WAS GOING TO HAMBURG WOULD SUIT US BEST.

I WENT TO GET PASSPORTS AND HERBERT WENT TO SEE STARTOP. WHEN WE MET AGAIN, HERBERT SAID STARTOP WANTED TO HELP US. WE ARRANGED THAT PROVIS WOULD COME DOWN TO THE STEPS BY THE HOUSE, ON WEDNESDAY, WHEN HE SAW US.

WHEN I GOT HOME, I FOUND A LETTER.

IF YOU WANT INFORMATION ABOUT PROVIS, COME TO THE HOUSE NEAR THE **KILN** ON THE **MARSHES** TONIGHT OR TOMORROW NIGHT.

TELL NO ONE.

COME ALONE.

I DECIDED TO GO. I LEFT A NOTE FOR HERBERT. I SAID I HAD GONE TO SEE MISS HAVISHAM.

I CAUGHT THE COACH AND WENT TO SATIS HOUSE. I WAS TOLD THAT MISS HAVISHAM WAS STILL VERY ILL.

I LOOKED IN MY POCKETS FOR THE LETTER BUT I COULD NOT FIND IT. HOWEVER, I KNEW THE PLACE WELL, AND SO I WENT OUT TO THE MARSHES.

VOLUME III
CHAPTER XIV

IT WAS A DARK NIGHT AND THE **MARSHES** WERE SAD AND EMPTY. I WALKED TOWARDS THE **KILN**.

I OPENED THE DOOR ...

CREEEEEAK...

NOW I'VE GOT YOU!

WHAT'S THIS?

HELP, HELP!

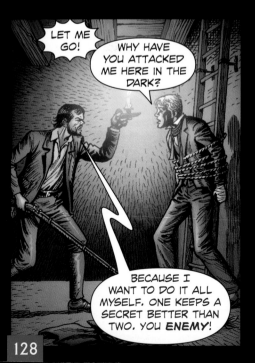

LET ME GO!

WHY HAVE YOU ATTACKED ME HERE IN THE DARK?

BECAUSE I WANT TO DO IT ALL MYSELF. ONE KEEPS A SECRET BETTER THAN TWO. YOU **ENEMY**!

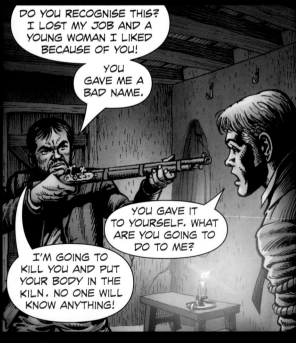

DO YOU RECOGNISE THIS? I LOST MY JOB AND A YOUNG WOMAN I LIKED BECAUSE OF YOU!

YOU GAVE ME A BAD NAME.

YOU GAVE IT TO YOURSELF. WHAT ARE YOU GOING TO DO TO ME?

I'M GOING TO KILL YOU AND PUT YOUR BODY IN THE KILN. NO ONE WILL KNOW ANYTHING!

I'M THE ONE THAT HIT YOUR SISTER. BUT IT WAS YOUR FAULT. YOU WERE THE FAVOURITE. NOW YOU'RE GOING TO PAY FOR IT.

gulp *gulp*

AND I'LL TELL YOU SOMETHING ELSE. IT WAS ME THAT YOU FELL OVER ON YOUR STAIRS THAT NIGHT. I'VE GOT SOME NEW *MASTERS*.

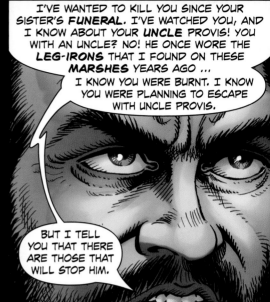

I'VE WANTED TO KILL YOU SINCE YOUR SISTER'S *FUNERAL*. I'VE WATCHED YOU, AND I KNOW ABOUT YOUR *UNCLE* PROVIS! YOU WITH AN UNCLE? NO! HE ONCE WORE THE *LEG-IRONS* THAT I FOUND ON THESE *MARSHES* YEARS AGO ...
I KNOW YOU WERE BURNT. I KNOW YOU WERE PLANNING TO ESCAPE WITH UNCLE PROVIS.

BUT I TELL YOU THAT THERE ARE THOSE THAT WILL STOP HIM.

HE PICKED UP A *HAMMER*. I SHOUTED AND FOUGHT AS HARD AS I COULD.

AARRGGHHH!!

GASP!

HA!

!

AARRRR!!

129

I **FAINTED** AND THEN WOKE AGAIN. I WAS LYING ON THE FLOOR WITH MY HEAD ON SOMEONE'S KNEE.

I THINK HE'S ALL RIGHT. HE'S VERY **PALE** THOUGH!

HERBERT!

AND STARTOP!

MY DEAR HANDEL, ARE YOU HURT? CAN YOU STAND?

YES, I CAN WALK. IT'S ONLY MY ARM THAT HURTS.

IT WAS RED AND EXTREMELY PAINFUL. THEY PUT NEW **BANDAGES** ON IT AND THEN WE LEFT.

I WANTED TO KNOW HOW THEY HAD FOUND ME. HERBERT SAID I HAD DROPPED THE LETTER IN OUR ROOMS AND HE HAD FOUND IT. HE AND STARTOP HAD COME AFTER ME AND HAD SPOKEN TO TRABB'S BOY. HE HAD SEEN ME WHEN I LEFT MISS HAVISHAM'S, AND HE TOOK THEM TO THE **KILN**.

WE DECIDED NOT TO CHASE ORLICK BECAUSE WE HAD TO GET BACK TO PROVIS. WE WENT BACK TO LONDON THAT NIGHT.

WE REACHED OUR ROOMS AND I WENT TO BED. I STAYED THERE ALL DAY.

MY ARM AND HEAD HURT, BUT AT LAST I FELL ASLEEP AND SLEPT DEEPLY.

VOLUME III CHAPTER XV IT WAS WEDNESDAY MORNING WHEN I LOOKED OUT OF THE WINDOW. I FELT STRONG AND WELL. STARTOP LAY ASLEEP ON THE SOFA. I MADE SOME COFFEE AND PACKED A BAG WITH A FEW THINGS.

WE PLANNED TO ROW UNTIL DARK. BY THEN WE WOULD BE PAST GRAVESEND. WE WERE GOING TO WAIT IN A QUIET **PUB** FOR THE NIGHT AND WAIT FOR THE SHIPS THAT WOULD LEAVE LONDON ON THURSDAY MORNING.

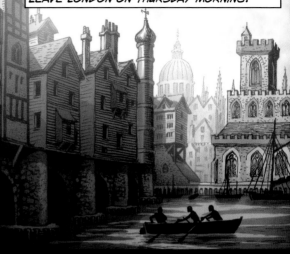

THANK YOU, DEAR BOY, THANK YOU!

I LOOKED FOR SIGNS OF PEOPLE WHO WERE WATCHING US, BUT I SAW NONE. I WAS ASHAMED THAT I COULDN'T ROW, BUT MY FRIENDS ROWED STRONGLY.

NIGHT FELL, AND WE ROWED ON FOR FOUR OR FIVE MILES. WE TIED UP THE BOAT BY A LONELY PUB, AND WENT IN. IT WAS DIRTY, BUT THERE WAS A FIRE AND TWO BEDROOMS.

WE GOT UP EARLY THE NEXT MORNING AND ROWED OUT INTO THE RIVER. AT HALF PAST ONE WE SAW TWO SHIPS.

WE GOT OUR BAGS READY AND SHOOK HANDS WITH EACH OTHER.

THEN ANOTHER BOAT SUDDENLY APPEARED FROM THE RIVER BANK.

THE BOAT CAME NEXT TO US. THE HAMBURG SHIP WAS ALMOST ON TOP OF US. SOMEONE SHOUTED TO US FROM THE BOAT.

YOU HAVE A RETURNED **PRISONER** THERE.

HIS NAME IS ABEL MAGWITCH. HE'S ALSO KNOWN AS PROVIS.

I ORDER HIM TO **SURRENDER**.

I FELL INTO THE WATER AND STAYED UNDER WATER FOR A FEW SECONDS ...

WHEN I CAME UP AGAIN I WAS TAKEN ONTO THE OTHER BOAT. HERBERT AND STARTOP WERE THERE, BUT THE TWO **PRISONERS** HAD GONE.

EVERYONE LOOKED AT THE WATER. SOON SOMETHING DARK SWAM TOWARDS US.

IT WAS MAGWITCH. HE WAS TAKEN ON BOARD AND **HANDCUFFS** WERE PUT ON HIM.

WE WENT TO THE **PUB** WE HAD LEFT EARLIER. I WAS ABLE TO GET SOME HELP HERE FOR MAGWITCH WHO WAS BADLY HURT IN THE **CHEST** AND HEAD. HE TOLD ME THAT HE AND COMPEYSON HAD FOUGHT UNDERWATER. HE HAD LEFT HIM AND SWUM AWAY.

I WENT WITH MAGWITCH TO LONDON ON THE BOAT. HERBERT AND STARTOP WENT BY LAND.

MAGWITCH'S BREATHING GOT WORSE AS NIGHT CAME. I THOUGHT IT WOULD BE BETTER FOR HIM TO DIE THEN. I DID NOT WANT HIM TO DIE LATER, AFTER A **TRIAL**.

MY DISLIKE OF HIM HAD GONE. IN HIM, I ONLY SAW A MAN WHO HAD MEANT TO HELP ME.

I TOLD HIM I WAS SAD THAT HE HAD COME HOME FOR ME.

DEAR BOY, I'M QUITE HAPPY. I'VE SEEN YOU, BUT DON'T TELL PEOPLE THAT YOU KNOW ME.

I WON'T LEAVE YOUR SIDE. I HOPE I'LL BE AS TRUE TO YOU AS YOU'VE BEEN TO ME!

I DECIDED NOT TO TELL HIM I WOULD NEVER BE RICH. HE WAS A PRISONER AGAIN; AND SO HE WOULD LOSE ALL HIS MONEY.

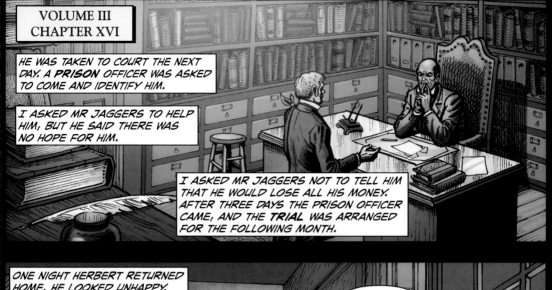

HE WAS TAKEN TO COURT THE NEXT DAY. A **PRISON** OFFICER WAS ASKED TO COME AND IDENTIFY HIM.

I ASKED MR JAGGERS TO HELP HIM, BUT HE SAID THERE WAS NO HOPE FOR HIM.

I ASKED MR JAGGERS NOT TO TELL HIM THAT HE WOULD LOSE ALL HIS MONEY. AFTER THREE DAYS THE PRISON OFFICER CAME, AND THE **TRIAL** WAS ARRANGED FOR THE FOLLOWING MONTH.

ONE NIGHT HERBERT RETURNED HOME. HE LOOKED UNHAPPY.

MY DEAR HANDEL, I'M AFRAID I'LL HAVE TO LEAVE YOU SOON. I MUST GO TO CAIRO. WE NEED A - A **CLERK** THERE. WILL YOU COME WITH ME AND TAKE THE JOB?

COULD I THINK ABOUT IT?

YES, OF COURSE.

THAT SATURDAY, I SAID GOODBYE TO HERBERT AND WENT BACK HOME. I FOUND WEMMICK THERE. I HADN'T SEEN HIM ALONE SINCE THE ATTEMPTED ESCAPE.

I HAVEN'T BEEN SO AFFECTED BY ANYTHING FOR A LONG TIME. I KEEP THINKING OF ALL THE MONEY HE'S LOST.

I KEEP THINKING OF THE POOR OWNER OF THE MONEY.

OF COURSE. BUT COMPEYSON WAS SO DETERMINED TO CATCH HIM THAT HE DIDN'T HAVE A CHANCE. I DID EVERYTHING I COULD FOR HIM, MR PIP.

I KNOW, AND I THANK YOU MOST WARMLY.

I'M TAKING A DAY'S HOLIDAY ON MONDAY, MR PIP. I'M GOING TO GO FOR A WALK, AND I'D LIKE YOU TO COME WITH ME.

I SAID I WOULD GO WITH HIM.

ON MONDAY MORNING WE WALKED TO CAMBERWELL GREEN.

HERE'S A CHURCH! LET'S GO IN!

HERE ARE SOME WHITE **GLOVES**! LET'S PUT THEM ON!

?

I BEGAN TO THINK I MIGHT BE AT A **WEDDING**.

I KNEW I WAS WHEN MISS SKIFFINS APPEARED IN A WEDDING DRESS.

HERE'S A RING! LET'S HAVE A WEDDING!

WHO GIVES THIS WOMAN TO THIS MAN?

FATHER, WHO GIVES HER?

ALL RIGHT, JOHN, ALL RIGHT, MY BOY!

WE HAD AN EXCELLENT BREAKFAST AND I DRANK TO THE NEW COUPLE, TO WEMMICK'S FATHER AND THE CASTLE.

MR PIP, THIS IS A WALWORTH OCCASION.

I UNDERSTAND. I WON'T MENTION IT IN LITTLE BRITAIN.

MR JAGGERS MIGHT THINK I WAS GOING SOFT. IT'S BEST IF HE DOESN'T KNOW ABOUT IT.

MAGWITCH WAS EXTREMELY ILL, SO HE WAS MOVED TO THE **PRISON** HOSPITAL. THIS GAVE ME MORE OPPORTUNITIES TO SEE HIM.

HIS **TRIAL** WAS VERY SHORT. HE HAD RETURNED TO THE COUNTRY AND SO HE WAS FOUND **GUILTY.**

ONE DAY AFTER HIS TRIAL, THIRTY-TWO MEN AND WOMEN WERE BROUGHT IN TO RECEIVE THEIR **SENTENCES.** MAGWITCH WAS ONE OF THEM.

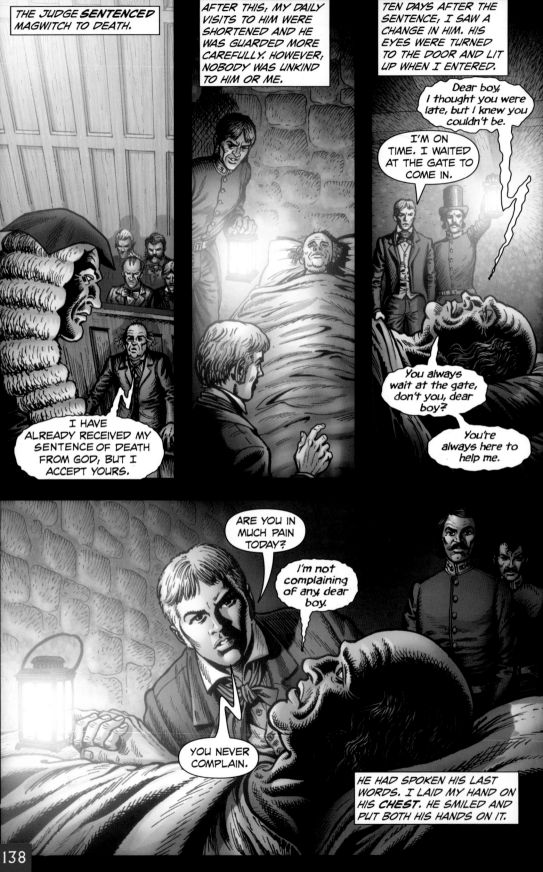

THE JUDGE **SENTENCED** MAGWITCH TO DEATH.

AFTER THIS, MY DAILY VISITS TO HIM WERE SHORTENED AND HE WAS GUARDED MORE CAREFULLY. HOWEVER, NOBODY WAS UNKIND TO HIM OR ME.

TEN DAYS AFTER THE SENTENCE, I SAW A CHANGE IN HIM. HIS EYES WERE TURNED TO THE DOOR AND LIT UP WHEN I ENTERED.

Dear boy, I thought you were late, but I knew you couldn't be.

I'M ON TIME. I WAITED AT THE GATE TO COME IN.

I HAVE ALREADY RECEIVED MY SENTENCE OF DEATH FROM GOD, BUT I ACCEPT YOURS.

You always wait at the gate, don't you, dear boy?

You're always here to help me.

ARE YOU IN MUCH PAIN TODAY?

I'm not complaining of any, dear boy.

YOU NEVER COMPLAIN.

HE HAD SPOKEN HIS LAST WORDS. I LAID MY HAND ON HIS **CHEST**. HE SMILED AND PUT BOTH HIS HANDS ON IT.

I WAS NOW ON MY OWN, AND I DECIDED TO LEAVE MY ROOMS. I WAS IN DEBT AND HAD VERY LITTLE MONEY. I DIDN'T FEEL WORRIED BECAUSE I WAS FALLING ILL.

FOR A DAY OR TWO, I LAY ON THE SOFA OR ON THE FLOOR – WHEREVER I FELL. MY BODY HURT AND I FELT VERY WEAK. I HAD A NIGHT FULL OF ANXIETY, AND IN THE MORNING I COULD NOT SIT UP.

SUDDENLY I SAW TWO MEN IN MY ROOM.

WHAT DO YOU WANT? I DON'T KNOW YOU.

WELL, SIR, YOU'RE **ARRESTED**. YOU **OWE** ONE HUNDRED AND TWENTY-THREE POUNDS TO A **JEWELLER**. YOU MUST COME TO MY HOUSE.

I TRIED TO GET UP AND DRESS MYSELF BUT COULDN'T. THEY WENT AWAY AND LEFT ME. I REMAINED VERY ILL FOR WHAT SEEMED AN ENDLESS TIME. HOWEVER, EVENTUALLY I BEGAN TO GET BETTER.

ONE DAY I OPENED MY EYES AND SAW IN THE CHAIR NEXT TO MY BED ...

IS IT JOE?

IT IS.

HOW LONG, DEAR JOE?

DO YOU MEAN HOW LONG HAVE YOU BEEN ILL? IT'S THE END OF MAY, OLD **CHAP**. WE WERE TOLD YOU WERE ILL IN A LETTER. I THOUGHT YOU WOULD BE AMONG STRANGERS AND THAT YOU WOULD LIKE A VISIT. BIDDY SAID I SHOULD COME TO YOU.

I WAITED UNTIL THE NEXT DAY TO ASK HIM ABOUT MISS HAVISHAM. WHEN I ASKED IF SHE WAS WELL, HE SHOOK HIS HEAD.

IS SHE DEAD?

SHE'S NOT LIVING, NO.

WHAT'S HAPPENED TO HER PROPERTY?

SHE LEFT MOST OF IT TO ESTELLA. BUT JUST BEFORE THE FIRE, SHE WROTE A NOTE IN WHICH SHE LEFT FOUR THOUSAND POUNDS TO MR MATTHEW POCKET.

AND ORLICK'S IN **PRISON**! HE ATTACKED PUMBLECHOOK IN HIS HOUSE.

I SLOWLY GOT STRONGER. JOE DID EVERYTHING FOR ME EXCEPT THE **HOUSEWORK**. HE PAID A WOMAN TO DO THAT.

WE **LOOKED FORWARD TO** THE DAY WHEN I COULD GO OUT. WHEN THE DAY CAME, WE DROVE INTO THE COUNTRY. EVERYWHERE WAS GREEN, AND THE SMELL OF SUMMER FILLED THE AIR.

I'M THANKFUL I WAS ILL, JOE.

DEAR PIP, YOU'RE ALMOST BETTER NOW.

I'LL NEVER FORGET THIS TIME WE'VE HAD TOGETHER.

THE NEXT MORNING, I WENT INTO JOE'S ROOM, BUT HE WAS NOT THERE. HE HAD LEFT A NOTE. OBVIOUSLY BIDDY HAD TAUGHT HIM TO WRITE.

I have left as you are well again, Dear Pip, And will do better without Joe.

P.S. Always the best of friends.

THERE WAS ALSO A PIECE OF PAPER FROM THE **JEWELLER**. JOE HAD PAID MY DEBT TO HIM.

I DECIDED TO GO TO THE **FORGE** TO TELL JOE ABOUT HOW I HAD NO MONEY. I WANTED TO TALK TO BIDDY TOO. I WANTED TO SHOW HER HOW SORRY I WAS.

I WANTED TO SAY TO HER, 'BIDDY, I THINK YOU LIKED ME ONCE. IF YOU CAN LIKE ME AGAIN, WILL YOU SPEND YOUR LIFE WITH ME?'

VOLUME III
CHAPTER XIX

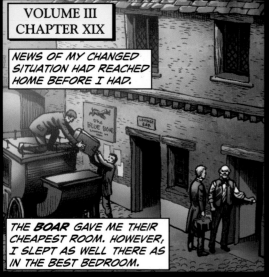

NEWS OF MY CHANGED SITUATION HAD REACHED HOME BEFORE I HAD.

THE **BOAR** GAVE ME THEIR CHEAPEST ROOM. HOWEVER, I SLEPT AS WELL THERE AS IN THE BEST BEDROOM.

EARLY THE NEXT MORNING I WALKED PAST SATIS HOUSE. THERE WAS A SIGN OUTSIDE. THE FURNITURE WAS GOING TO BE SOLD THE FOLLOWING WEEK. THE HOUSE WAS GOING TO BE SOLD AND PULLED DOWN.

Saturday 3rd May
FOR SALE BY PUBLIC
AUCTION
SATIS HOUSE

WHEN I GOT BACK TO THE BOAR FOR BREAKFAST, I FOUND MR PUMBLECHOOK.

YOUNG MAN, I'M SORRY TO HEAR YOUR NEWS. BUT WHAT COULD YOU EXPECT! ARE YOU GOING TO SEE JOSEPH?

WHY DO YOU CARE WHERE I AM GOING?

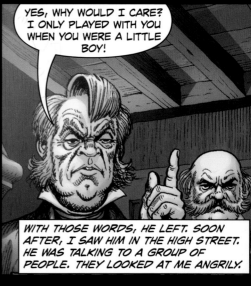

YES, WHY WOULD I CARE? I ONLY PLAYED WITH YOU WHEN YOU WERE A LITTLE BOY!

WITH THOSE WORDS, HE LEFT. SOON AFTER, I SAW HIM IN THE HIGH STREET. HE WAS TALKING TO A GROUP OF PEOPLE. THEY LOOKED AT ME ANGRILY.

AT LAST I SAW THE **FORGE**. IT WAS CLOSED. I WENT TOWARDS THE HOUSE AND THEN SUDDENLY JOE AND BIDDY WERE STANDING IN FRONT OF ME. BIDDY GAVE A **CRY** AND I PUT MY ARMS AROUND HER.

YOU BOTH LOOK SO SMART!

YES, DEAR PIP.

IT'S MY **WEDDING** DAY, AND I'M MARRIED TO JOE!

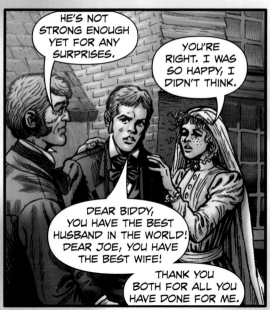

HE'S NOT STRONG ENOUGH YET FOR ANY SURPRISES.

YOU'RE RIGHT. I WAS SO HAPPY, I DIDN'T THINK.

DEAR BIDDY, YOU HAVE THE BEST HUSBAND IN THE WORLD! DEAR JOE, YOU HAVE THE BEST WIFE!

THANK YOU BOTH FOR ALL YOU HAVE DONE FOR ME.

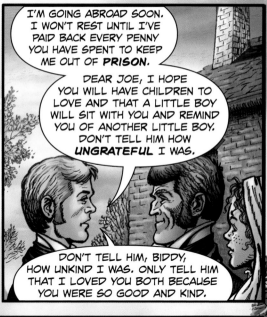

I'M GOING ABROAD SOON. I WON'T REST UNTIL I'VE PAID BACK EVERY PENNY YOU HAVE SPENT TO KEEP ME OUT OF **PRISON**.

DEAR JOE, I HOPE YOU WILL HAVE CHILDREN TO LOVE AND THAT A LITTLE BOY WILL SIT WITH YOU AND REMIND YOU OF ANOTHER LITTLE BOY. DON'T TELL HIM HOW **UNGRATEFUL** I WAS.

DON'T TELL HIM, BIDDY, HOW UNKIND I WAS. ONLY TELL HIM THAT I LOVED YOU BOTH BECAUSE YOU WERE SO GOOD AND KIND.

PLEASE TELL ME THAT YOU **FORGIVE** ME!

OH, DEAR OLD PIP, I FORGIVE YOU, IF I HAVE ANYTHING TO FORGIVE!

I DO TOO!

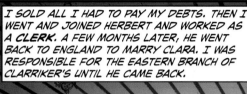

I SOLD ALL I HAD TO PAY MY DEBTS. THEN I WENT AND JOINED HERBERT AND WORKED AS A **CLERK**. A FEW MONTHS LATER, HE WENT BACK TO ENGLAND TO MARRY CLARA. I WAS RESPONSIBLE FOR THE EASTERN BRANCH OF CLARRIKER'S UNTIL HE CAME BACK.

MANY YEARS PASSED AND I LIVED HAPPILY WITH HERBERT AND CLARA. I WROTE REGULARLY TO BIDDY AND JOE. WHEN I BECAME A PARTNER IN CLARRIKER'S, CLARRIKER TOLD HERBERT WHAT I HAD DONE FOR HIM. HERBERT WAS VERY MOVED.

WE WERE NOT A **GRAND** BUSINESS, BUT WE HAD A GOOD NAME, AND WE DID VERY WELL.

143

I HAD NOT SEEN JOE OR BIDDY FOR ELEVEN YEARS, WHEN I WENT BACK TO THE *FORGE*.

I LOOKED THROUGH THE DOOR, AND JOE WAS SITTING THERE, AND A LITTLE BOY!

WE CALLED HIM PIP, AFTER YOU, OLD *CHAP*. WE THINK HE'S A LITTLE BIT LIKE YOU.

BIDDY, YOU MUST LEND HIM TO ME ONE DAY.

NO, NO, YOU MUST MARRY.

I DON'T THINK I WILL.

DEAR PIP, DO YOU STILL LOVE HER?

NO, I DON'T THINK SO.

HAVE YOU FORGOTTEN HER?

I HAVEN'T FORGOTTEN ANYTHING THAT WAS IMPORTANT, BUT THAT DREAM HAS GONE.

HOWEVER, I INTENDED TO VISIT THE PLACE WHERE THE OLD HOUSE HAD STOOD. AND I KNEW THAT MY VISIT WOULD BE BECAUSE OF ESTELLA.

I HAD HEARD THAT ESTELLA HAD BEEN VERY UNHAPPY. HER HUSBAND HAD BEEN EXTREMELY UNKIND TO HER AND SHE HAD LEFT HIM.

HE HAD DIED IN A RIDING ACCIDENT TWO YEARS EARLIER. SHE COULD BE MARRIED AGAIN – I DIDN'T KNOW.

IN THE COLD *MIST*, I SAW SOMEONE ...

PIP!

ESTELLA!

I'M SURPRISED YOU RECOGNISE ME.

THE FRESHNESS OF HER BEAUTY HAD GONE, BUT SHE WAS STILL LOVELY. HER EYES, THAT HAD BEEN PROUD, WERE NOW SOFT AND SAD.

AFTER SO MANY YEARS, IT'S STRANGE TO MEET YOU HERE, ESTELLA! DO YOU OFTEN COME BACK?

I'VE OFTEN WANTED TO COME BACK, BUT HAVEN'T BEEN ABLE TO. THE GROUND HERE IS ALL THAT I HAVE KEPT FROM WHAT I *INHERITED*. IT'S THE ONLY THING I FOUGHT FOR.

I HAVE OFTEN THOUGHT OF YOU. SINCE MY HUSBAND DIED, THE MEMORY OF WHAT I THREW AWAY HAS HAD A PLACE IN MY HEART.

YOU HAVE ALWAYS HAD A PLACE IN *MY* HEART.

I DIDN'T THINK I WOULD HAVE TO SAY GOODBYE TO YOU TONIGHT. BUT I'M VERY HAPPY TO DO SO.

HAPPY TO **PART** AGAIN? THE MEMORY OF OUR LAST PARTING IS STILL PAINFUL TO ME.

BUT YOU SAID TO ME, 'I PRAY THAT GOD **FORGIVES** YOU!' IF YOU COULD SAY IT THEN, YOU'LL BE ABLE TO SAY IT NOW, NOW THAT I AM BROKEN.

TELL ME WE ARE FRIENDS.

WE'RE FRIENDS.

AND ALWAYS WILL BE.

I TOOK HER HAND IN MINE AND WE LEFT THE RUINED PLACE.

THE EVENING **MISTS** WERE RISING, AND IN THE PEACEFUL LIGHT I SAW NO SHADOW OF ANOTHER PARTING FROM HER.

GREAT EXPECTATIONS

The End

Glossary

A

accountant /əˈkaʊntənt/ – (accountants) An accountant is a person whose job is to keep financial accounts.

adopt (a child) /əˈdɒt/ – (adopts, adopting, adopted) If you adopt someone else's child, you take it into your own family, and make it legally your own.

affairs /əˈfeəs/ – Your affairs are your own personal concerns.

apprentice /əˈprentɪs/ – (apprentices) An apprentice is a person who works with someone in order to learn their skill.

agent /ˈeɪdʒənt/ – (agents) An agent is someone who arranges work or business for someone else.

arrest /əˈrest/ – (arrests, arresting, arrested) When the police arrest someone or make an arrest, they take them to a police station in order to decide whether they should be charged with an offence. *Police arrested five young men in connection with the attacks.*

awful /ˈɔːfʊl/ If you say that something is awful, you mean that it is very bad. *Her injuries were massive. It was awful.*

B

bandage /ˈbændɪdʒ/ – (bandages) A bandage is a long strip of cloth that is tied around a wounded part of someone's body in order to protect or support it.

bang /bæŋ/ A bang is a sudden loud noise such as an explosion.

battery /ˈbætəri/ A battery is an area where large guns were placed during the war.

beer /bɪə/ – (beers) Beer is a bitter alcoholic drink made from grain. A beer is a glass of beer.

bell /bel/ – (bells) A bell is a device that makes a ringing sound which attracts people's attention. *I've been ringing the door bell.*

benefactor /ˈbenɪfæktə/ – (benefactors) Your benefactor is a person who helps you by giving you money.

blacksmith /ˈblæksmɪθ/ – (blacksmiths) A blacksmith is someone whose job is making things out of metal, for example horseshoes.

blind /blaɪnd/ - (blinds) If you are blind, you cannot see because your eyes are damaged. *He went blind.* A blind is a roll of material which you pull down over a window to keep out the light.

boar /bɔː/ – (boars) A boar or a wild boar is a wild pig. A male pig is also known as a boar.

(brandy column)

brandy /ˈbrændi/ Brandy is a strong alcoholic drink.

brewery /ˈbruːəri/ – (breweries) A brewery is a place where beer is made.

bride /braɪd/ – (brides) A bride is a woman who is getting married or who has just got married. *The guests crowded around the bride and groom.*

bring (somebody) up /brɪŋ ʌp/ – (brought up) If you bring up a child, you look after it until it is grown up.

C

carol /ˈkærəl/ – (carols) Carols are Christian religious songs that are sung at Christmas.

ceiling /ˈsiːlɪŋ/ – (ceilings) A ceiling is the top inside surface of a room. *... a small air vent in the ceiling.*

chap /tʃæp/ – (chaps) A chap is a man or boy.

cheek /tʃiːk/ – (cheeks) Your cheeks are the sides of your face below your eyes.

cheque /tʃek/ – (cheques) A cheque is a printed form on which you write an amount of money and say who it is to be paid to. Your bank then pays the money to that person from your account. *He wrote them a cheque for £10,000. / I'd like to pay by cheque.*

chest /tʃest/ – (chests) Your chest is the top part of the front of your body. *He was shot in the chest.*

churchyard /ˈtʃɜːtʃjɑːd/ – (churchyards) A churchyard is the enclosed ground around a church. It is used especially for burials.

clerk /klɑːk/ – (clerks) A clerk is a person who works in an office, bank, or law court and whose job is to look after records or accounts.

cough /kɒf/ – (coughs, coughing, coughed) When you cough, you force air out of your throat with a sudden harsh noise. A cough is an act of coughing. *Graham began to cough. / She heard a loud cough behind her.*

counting-house /ˈkaʊntɪŋ haʊs/ – (counting-houses) A counting-house is a place people keep their accounts and where accountants work.

courtyard /ˈkɔːtjɑːd/ – (courtyards) A courtyard is a flat open area of ground surrounded by buildings or walls.

cross /krɒs/ – (crosses, crossing, crossed) If you cross a room, road or area of land, you move to the other side of it. *She stood up and crossed to the door.* If you cross your arms, legs or fingers, you put one of them on top of the other. *Paul crossed his arms over his chest.*

cry /kraɪ/ – (cries) A cry is a loud high sound that you make when you feel a strong emotion such as fear, pain or pleasure. *... a cry of horror.*

D

daylight /ˈdeɪlaɪt/ Daylight is the light that there is during the day, or the time of day when it is light. *It was still daylight. / Paul returned shortly after daylight.*

deaf /def/ – Deaf people or the deaf are unable to hear anything or unable to hear very well. *She is deaf. / Many regular TV programmes are captioned for the deaf.*

deer /dɪə/ A deer is a large wild animal. Male deer usually have large, branching horns.

dull /dʌl/ A dull colour or light is not bright. *The stamp was a dark, dull blue colour.*

dust /dʌst/ Dust consists of very small dry particles of earth, sand or dirt. *I could see a thick layer of dust on the stairs.*

E

enemy /ˈenəmi/ – (enemies) Your enemy is someone who intends to harm you.

evidence /ˈevɪdəns/ Evidence is anything that makes you believe that something is true or exists. *There is no evidence to support this.*

expectations /ˌekspekˈteɪʃəns/ In Victorian times your expectations were your prospects of inheritance.

F

faint /feɪnt/ – (faints, fainting, fainted) If you faint, or if you fall into a faint, you lose consciousness for a short time.

file /faɪl/ – (files) A file is a tool with rough surfaces, used for smoothing and shaping hard materials.

find (someone) guilty /faɪnd ˈgɪlti/ When a court or jury finds someone guilty of doing something bad or committing a crime, they have done a bad thing or committed a crime. *He was found guilty of causing death by dangerous driving.*

find (someone) innocent /faɪnd ˈɪnəsənt/ When a court or jury finds someone innocent, they did not commit a crime which they have been accused of. *The man was found innocent of murder.*

fire /faɪə/ – (fires, firing, fired) If someone fires, or fires a gun or a bullet, a bullet is sent from a gun that they are using. You can refer to the shots fired as *fire*.

flap /flæp/ – (flaps) A flap of cloth or skin is a flat piece of it that moves freely because it is attached by only one edge.

flat /flæt/ – (flatter, flattest) Something that is flat is level and smooth. *The sea was calm, perfectly flat.*

fond /fɒnd/ – (fonder, fondest) If you are fond of someone or something, you like that person or thing. *I am very fond of Michael.*

footstep /ˈfʊtstep/ – (footsteps) A footstep is the sound made by someone's feet touching the ground when they are walking or running. *They heard footsteps in the main room.*

forge /fɔːdʒ/ – (forges) A forge is a place where a blacksmith makes metal things such as horseshoes.

forgive /fəˈgɪv/ – (forgives, forgiving, forgave, forgiven) If you forgive someone who has done something wrong, you stop being angry with them. *She forgave him for stealing her money.*

forbidden /fəˈbɪdən/ If something is forbidden, you are not allowed to do it or have it. *Eating was forbidden. / It is forbidden to drive faster than 20 mph.*

forgiveness /fəˈgɪvnɪs/ When you forgive someone, they get your forgiveness. *He fell to his knees and begged for forgiveness.*

fortune /ˈfɔːtʃuːn/ – (fortunes) Fortune or good fortune is good luck. A fortune is a large amount of money.

funeral /ˈfjuːnərəl/ – (funerals) A funeral is a ceremony for someone who has died. *His funeral will be on Thursday at Blackburn Cathedral.*

G

gentleman /ˈdʒentəlmən/ – (gentlemen) A gentleman is a man from a family of high social standing. *The traditional country gentleman.* A gentleman is a man who is polite and well-educated. *He was always such a gentleman.*

glove /glʌv/ – (gloves) Gloves are pieces of clothing which cover your hand and wrist and have individual sections for each finger.

grand /grænd/ – (grander, grandest) If you describe something as grand you mean that it is splendid and impressive.

grateful /ˈgreɪtful/ – (gratefully) If you are grateful for something that someone has given you or done for you, you are pleased and wish to thank them. *I am grateful to you for your help./ I gratefully accepted the offer.*

great-aunt /ˈgreɪtɑːnt/ – (great-aunts) Your great-aunt is the sister of your grandmother or grandfather.

guilty /ˈgɪlti/ - (guiltier, guiltiest) If someone is guilty of doing something bad or committing a crime, they have done a bad thing or committed a crime. *He was found guilty of causing death by dangerous driving. / If someone is guilty, he should be punished.*

gun /gʌn/ – (guns) A gun is a weapon from which bullets or pellets are fired.

H

hammer /ˈhæmə/ – (hammers) A hammer is a tool used for hitting things. It consists of a heavy piece of metal at the end of a handle.

handcuff /'hændkʌf/ – (handcuffs) Handcuffs are two metal rings linked by a short chain which are locked round a prisoner's wrists. *He was led away to jail in handcuffs.*

hang /hæŋ/ – (hangs, hanging, hanged) If someone is hanged, they are killed by having a rope tied around their neck and the support taken away from under their feet. *He was hanged last month for murder.*

heaven /'hevən/ – (heavens) You say *good heavens* to express surprise. *Good heavens! That explains a lot!*

horrible /'hɒrɪbəl/ If you say that someone or something is horrible, you mean that they are very unpleasant. *... a horrible small boy.*

housekeeper /'haʊskiːpə/ – (housekeepers) A housekeeper is a person employed to do the cleaning and cooking in a house.

housework /'haʊswɜːk/ Housework is the work such as cleaning and cooking that you do in your home.

hut /hʌt/ – (huts) A hut is a small, simple building, often made of wood, mud or grass.

I

inherit /ɪn'herɪt/ – (inherits, inheriting, inherited) If you inherit money or property, you receive it from someone who has died. *He inherited these paintings from his father.*

inn /ɪn/ – (inns) An inn is a small hotel or a pub, usually an old one.

innocent /'ɪnəsənt/ If someone is innocent, they did not commit a crime which they have been accused of. *He was sure that the man was innocent of murder.*

J

jealous /'dʒeləs/ If you are jealous of another person's possessions or qualities, you feel angry or bitter because you do not have them. *She was jealous of his well-paid job.*

jewel /'dʒuːəl/ – (jewels) A jewel is a precious stone used to decorate valuable things such as rings or necklaces. *The jewels in the collection include sapphires and a huge diamond.*

jeweller /'dʒuːələ/ – (jewellers) A jeweller is a person who makes, sells and repairs jewellery and watches.

jewellery /'dʒuːəlri/ Jewellery consists of ornaments that people wear such as rings and bracelets.

K

kiln /kɪln/ – (kilns) A kiln is an oven that is used to bake pottery and bricks in order to make them hard.

L

leg-iron /'legaɪən/ – (leg-irons) A leg-iron is a ring made of iron used for holding a prisoner by the ankles.

look forward to /lʊk 'fɔːwəd tə/ If you look forward to something, you want it to happen because you think you will enjoy it. *I'm really looking forward to meeting him.*

M

ma'am /mæm, maːm/ People sometimes say *ma'am* as a formal and polite way of addressing a woman.

marsh /maːʃ/ – (marshes) A marsh is a wet muddy area of land.

master /'maːstə, 'mæstə/ – (masters) A servant's master is the man that he or she works for.

miserable /'mɪzərəbəl/ – (miserably) If you are miserable, you are very unhappy.

mist /mɪst/ Mist consists of many tiny drops of water in the air, which make it difficult to see very far. *I couldn't see anything through the mist.*

O

object /'ɒbdʒɪkt/ – (objects, objecting, objected) If you object to something, you express your dislike or disapproval of it. *Working people everywhere object to paying taxes.*

odd /ɒd/ – (odder, oddest) If you say that someone or something is odd, you mean that they are strange or unusual. *He'd always been odd. / He used to wear rather odd clothes.*

owe /əʊ/ – (owes, owing, owed) If you owe money to someone, they have lent it to you and you have not yet paid it back. *The company owes money to more than 60 banks.*

P

pale /peɪl/ – (paler, palest) If someone looks pale, their face is a lighter colour than usual, because they are ill, frightened or shocked.

part /paːt/ – (parts, parting, parted) When two people part, they leave each other or separate. *He is going to part from his wife.*

passage /'pæsɪdʒ/ – (passages) A passage is a long, narrow space between walls or fences connecting one room or place with another.

poker /'pəʊkə/ A poker is a metal stick used to make pushing movements at an open fire.

prison /'prɪzən/ – (prisons) A prison is a building where criminals are kept.

prisoner /'prɪzənə/ – (prisoners) A prisoner is a person who is kept in a prison as a punishment.

pub /pʌb/ – (pubs) A pub is a building where people can buy and drink alcoholic drinks.

R

revenge /rɪ'vendʒ/ — Revenge involves hurting someone who has hurt you. *Acts of revenge. / The other children took revenge on the boy, claiming he was a school bully. / They said that the attack was in revenge for the killing of their leader.*

rob /rɒb/ — (robs, robbing, robbed) If a person or place is robbed, money or property is stolen from them, often using force. *He was arrested after robbing a bank.*

robbery /'rɒbəri/ — (robberies) Robbery is the crime of stealing money or property, often using force. *The gang committed dozens of armed robberies.*

rude /ruːd/ — (ruder, rudest) If someone is rude, they behave in a way that is not polite. *He's rude to her friends.*

rum /rʌm/ — Rum is an alcoholic drink made from sugar cane juice.

S

sedan chair /sɪ'dæn tʃeə/ — (sedan chairs) A sedan chair is an enclosed chair for one person carried on two poles by two men, one in front and one behind.

sentence /'sentəns/ — (sentences, sentencing, sentenced) A sentence is the punishment that a person receives after they have been found guilty of a crime. *He served a prison sentence for bank robbery.* When judges sentence someone, they state in court what the person's punishment will be. *The court sentenced him to five years' imprisonment.*

shilling /'ʃɪlɪŋ/ — (shillings) A shilling is a former British coin worth twelve pence or one-twentieth of a pound.

smash /smæʃ/ — (smashes, smashing, smashed) If something smashes or is smashed against something solid, it moves with great force against it. *He smashed his fist into Anthony's face.*

spirit /'spɪrɪt/ A person's spirit is a part of them that is not physical and that is believed to remain alive after their death.

spoil /spɔɪl/ — (spoils, spoiling, spoiled or spoilt) If you say that someone spoils their children, you mean that they give their children everything they want and that this has a bad effect on their character.

stupid /'stjuːpɪd/ — (stupider, stupidest) If you say that someone or something is stupid, you mean that they show a lack of good judgement or intelligence and they are not at all sensible. *How could I have been so stupid? / I made a stupid mistake.*

surrender /sə'rendə/ — (surrenders, surrendering, surrendered) If you surrender, you stop fighting or resisting someone or something and agree that you have been beaten. Surrender is the act of surrendering.

T

tame /teɪm/ — (tames, taming, tamed) If someone tames a wild animal or bird, they train it not to be afraid of humans.

tar /taː/ Tar is a thick, black, sticky substance used in making roads.

thud /θʌd/ (thuds) A thud is a dull sound, usually made by a solid, heavy object hitting something soft. *She tripped and fell with a sickening thud.*

torch /tɔːtʃ/ — (torches) A torch is a long stick with burning material at one end, used to provide light or to set things on fire.

town hall /taʊn hɔːl/ — (town halls) The town hall in a town is a large building owned and used by the town council, often as its headquarters.

trial /traɪəl/ — (trials) A trial is the legal process in which a judge and jury listen to evidence and decide whether a person is guilty of a crime. *He was giving evidence at the trial of Gary Hart, aged 37.*

try /traɪ/ — (tries, trying, tried) When a person is tried, they appear in court and are found innocent or guilty after the judge and jury have heard the evidence.

U

uncle /'ʌŋkəl/ — (uncles) Your uncle is the brother of your mother or father, or the husband of your aunt.

uncommon /ʌn'kɒmən/ If you describe someone as uncommon you mean that they are special and not ordinary.

ungrateful /ʌn'greɪtfəl/ If you describe someone as ungrateful, you are criticising them for not showing thanks or for being unkind to someone who has helped them or done them a favour. *I thought it was ungrateful of her.*

W

watchman /'wɒtʃmən/ — (watchmen) A watchman is a person whose job is to guard a building or area.

wedding /'wedɪŋ/ — (weddings) A wedding is a marriage ceremony and the celebration that often takes place afterwards.

wine /waɪn/ — (wines) Wine is an alcoholic drink, usually made from grapes.

wrist /rɪst/ — (wrists) Your wrist is the part of your body between your hand and arm which bends when you move your hand.

Character Summary

Pip

The main character and narrator. He starts the story as a young orphan being looked after by his sister and her husband. Pip is a passionate and romantic boy who is sometimes unrealistic in what he expects. Pip is very conscientious. He wants to improve himself morally and socially.

Estella

A beautiful young dependant who is being looked after by Miss Havisham. Pip loves Estella passionately. However, while Estella sometimes seems to consider him a friend, she is usually cold and cruel. As they grow up together, she warns him again and again that she has no heart.

Miss Havisham

A wealthy, strange old woman who lives in a manor called Satis House near Pip's village. She often seems insane: she wears only an old wedding dress, keeps a rotting feast on her table and surrounds herself with clocks all stopped at twenty minutes to nine. As a young woman, Miss Havisham was left by her fiancé minutes before her wedding. Now she hates all men.

Abel Magwitch ('The Convict')

A criminal, Magwitch escapes from prison at the beginning of *Great Expectations* and frightens Pip in the cemetery. Pip's kindness, however, impresses him. After he makes a fortune, he uses it to help Pip. He becomes Pip's secret supporter and pays for Pip's education and lifestyle in London.

Joe Gargery

Pip's brother-in-law. He is the village blacksmith. Joe stays with his bossy, violent wife because he loves Pip. Although Joe is uneducated and unrefined, he lives for those he loves through his quiet goodness.

Jaggers

A powerful lawyer hired by Magwitch to look after Pip. Jaggers is one of the most important criminal lawyers in London and many criminals are terrified of him.

Herbert Pocket

He dares Pip to a fight in the garden of Satis House when they are children. Years later, they meet again in London. Herbert becomes Pip's best friend after Pip becomes a gentleman.

Wemmick

Jaggers's clerk and Pip's friend. At work, Wemmick is a hard and sarcastic man. At home, however, he is a happy and tender caretaker of his 'Aged Parent.'

Character Summary

Biddy

A kind-hearted country girl. She and Pip become friends at school. After Mrs Joe is attacked and becomes an invalid, Biddy moves into Pip's home to care for her. Biddy is the opposite of Estella; she is plain, kind and moral.

Dolge Orlick

The day labourer in Joe's forge. He is an evil and hateful man who hurts people because he enjoys it.

Mrs Joe

Pip's sister and Joe's wife. She is a stern and overbearing figure. She keeps a very clean household and often threatens her husband and her brother with her cane, which she calls 'Tickler.' Mrs Joe is petty and ambitious.

Uncle Pumblechook

Pip's pompous, arrogant uncle. A merchant obsessed with money, Pumblechook is responsible for organising Pip's first meeting with Miss Havisham.

Molly

Jaggers's housekeeper. Pip realises that she is Estella's mother.

Mr Wopsle

The church clerk in Pip's country town. After Pip becomes a gentleman, Mr Wopsle moves to London and becomes an actor.

Startop

A friend of Pip's and Herbert's. Startop is a frail young man who studies with Pip.

Miss Skiffins

Wemmick's much-loved and eventual wife.

Charles Dickens's Life

Charles Dickens was born on February 7, 1812. He lived near the sea in south-east England until he was nine years old. He was the second of eight children born to John and Elizabeth Dickens. Dickens's father, John, was a kind and likable man. However, he was not very good with money and made many debts throughout his life. The Dickens family were comfortable for a while, and sent Dickens to a fee-paying school when he was nine. By the time he was ten, however, they moved to London, and when he was 12 his father was arrested and taken to debtors' prison.

Dickens's mother and his seven brothers and sisters moved into prison with their father, which was common at the time. Mrs Dickens arranged for young Charles to live alone outside the prison and work with other children. He pasted labels on bottles in a blacking warehouse (blacking was a type of manufactured soot used to make a black pigment for products such as matches). Dickens found the three months he spent apart from his family very distressing. Not only did he hate the job, but he considered himself too good for it. He never forgot this terrible experience. His mother died soon after and left enough money to pay off the debts and get his father released from prison.

Once his father was allowed out of prison, Dickens returned to school. He eventually became a law clerk, and then a court reporter. From 1830 to 1836 Dickens wrote for a number of newspapers as a journalist. In 1833 his first published story, *A Dinner at Poplar Walk,* was published. Soon after, he began to write 'his series' for *The Chronicle.*

On April 2nd, 1836, Charles Dickens married Catherine Hogarth (the daughter of his editor, George Hogarth). They had ten children (seven boys and three girls). Also in 1836, Dickens published the first series of *Sketches by Boz.* ('Boz' was a pen name used by Dickens).

After this, Dickens finally became a full-time novelist. His first novel, *The Pickwick Papers,* became a huge popular success when Dickens was only 25. He wrote novels very quickly, writing *Oliver Twist* as a monthly series between 1837 and 1839. In 1843, his dearly loved Christmas tale, *A Christmas Carol*, was published. It sold 5,000 copies on Christmas Eve – and has never been out of print since.

Unfortunately, Dickens's personal life was not as successful. He separated from his wife Catherine in 1858, and denied having an affair. Although his work promoted family values, Dickens appears to have been having an affair with an actress called Ellen Lawless Ternan. He tried very hard to keep his personal life private.

However, Dickens continued to publish extensively. He became well known internationally, travelling to Canada and the United States twice as well as Europe. He gave many public readings of his works, even after his doctors started to advise him to rest. Dickens didn't listen: he began work on one last novel, *The Mystery of Edwin Drood*. This work was never finished, for Dickens suffered a stroke and died suddenly on 9th June, 1870.

Although Charles Dickens asked to be buried in a simple and private manner, he was so popular that the public insisted he was recognised as a great writer. He was buried at Westminster Abbey. His funeral, however, was private, with only 12 people present. After the service, thousands of people came to pay their respects. Today, a small stone marks his grave and simply says:
'Charles Dickens
Born 7th February 1812
Died 9th June 1870'.

The Context of Great Expectations

Many of the events from Charles Dickens's early life are echoed in *Great Expectations*. It is one of his most autobiographical novels. Pip, the main character, lives in the marsh country. He works at a job he hates and considers himself too good for his surroundings. He also experiences material success in London at a very early age, just as Dickens himself did. In addition, the law, justice and the courts are all important parts of the story. One of the novel's most engaging characters, Wemmick, is a law clerk.

Great Expectations is set in early Victorian England. It was a period when great social changes were spreading across the nation. The Industrial Revolution of the late eighteenth and early nineteenth centuries had completely changed the social landscape. Manufacturers could become very rich. Yet although social class was no longer depended entirely on your birth, the divisions between rich and poor remained almost as wide as ever. Dark and smoky London was very different to England's thinly populated rural areas. More and more people moved from the country to the city in search of money.

With the increase in population, London also increased in crime. To fight against the increase in crime, the government strengthened the law. Many crimes became punished with death — even small crimes of theft. Prisoners were hanged in public. Dickens himself was among the protestors who helped stop public hangings in 1868.

Newgate Prison is an important place in *Great Expectations*. It was not only the main prison in London, but also a symbol of crime itself. In various forms, a prison had existed on the site since 1300. In the eighteenth-century, the prison was divided into three areas: an area for debtors (people who owed money), male criminals and female criminals. While debtors lived there long-term, the other criminals were usually only there while they were waiting for trial, execution or transportation to the colonies. The latter were usually held in prison hulks on the River Thames until they were transported. The prison hulks were well-known for their terrible conditions. The decks were divided into caged cells, and prisoners were forced to sleep with chains around their waists and ankles. The hulks were places of diseases such as cholera and dysentery.

Given the overcrowding of the hulks, over 150,000 convicts were sent to the British colony of Australia between 1788 and 1868. Many prisoners, like Abel Magwitch, served only a short sentence and went on to make a fortune in the new land.

All of these conditions characterised Dickens's time as well as the storyline of *Great Expectations*. Pip's sudden rise from a worker in the country to a gentleman in the city forces him to move from one extreme to another. He also has to cope with the strict rules and expectations that controlled Victorian England. Ironically, this novel about wanting wealth and social advancement was written partly from Dickens's own economic necessity. Dickens needed the money because his magazine was no longer as popular as it had once been.

Great Expectations belongs to the bildungsroman (or novel depicting growth and personal development) which was a popular pattern in nineteenth-century European fiction. The story shows Pip's change from boyhood to manhood.

A Tale With Two Endings?

The ending of *Great Expectations* is more controversial than many readers realise. Before writing the scene in which Pip finds Estella in the garden and sees 'no shadow of another parting from her,' Dickens wrote a different ending to the book. It was much less romantic.

In this original version, Pip hears that, after Drummle's death, Estella married a country doctor in Shropshire. Walking through London one day with Joe and Biddy's son, Pip sees Estella. They have a very brief meeting and shake hands. Although they don't discuss what happened in the past, Pip says he could see that 'suffering had been stronger than Miss Havisham's teaching and had given her a heart to understand what my heart used to be.'

Dickens changed this ending because his friend, the novelist Edward Bulwer Lytton, suggested he do so. It seems that he wanted his reading public to have a happier ending. However, many critics think that the original ending is better because it is more true to the novel's tone. However, others think the second ending is better because the entire story is about the development of each of these two characters, which can finally be realised in their love for each other.

In every reprint of the novel, Dickens kept the final version. Yet the original ending, changed only due to his friend's influence, was Dickens's first sense of how the story should end. Though the romantic ending remains the 'official' ending of the book, each reader of *Great Expectations* may interpret the novel for themselves, and decide which ending best fits their own understanding of *Great Expectations*.

Important Quotations

1 'My convict looked round him for the first time, and saw me ... I looked at him eagerly when he looked at me, and slightly moved my hands and shook my head. I had been waiting for him to see me, that I might try to assure him of my innocence. It was not at all expressed to me that he even comprehended my intention, for he gave me a look that I did not understand, and it all passed in a moment. But if he had looked at me for an hour or for a day, I could not have remembered his face ever afterwards as having been more attentive.'

This quotation describes Pip's short meeting with Magwitch who had just been recaptured by the police. Pip wants Magwitch to know that he is innocent; that he didn't tell the police about Magwitch. The quotation is important for two reasons. First, it shows how very concerned Pip is about what people think of him. Secondly, it hints about what is to occur in the novel: Magwitch feels loyalty and love for Pip, who has been very kind to him. We see that Magwitch is not an entirely bad person.

2 'Pip, dear old chap, life is made of ever so many partings welded together, as I may say, and one man's a blacksmith, and one's a whitesmith, and one's a goldsmith, and one's a coppersmith. Divisions among such must come, and must be met as they come.'

Joe says these words to Pip as a farewell after they meet awkwardly in London. Pip is now a gentleman. He is embarrassed by both Joe's commonness and his own luxurious lifestyle. With this quotation, Joe tells Pip that he does not blame him for the awkwardness, but instead states that it is due to natural divisions in life. In this simple way, Joe arrives at a wise and resigned attitude toward the changes in Pip's social class that have divided them.

3 'So,' said Estella, 'I must be taken as I have been made. The success is not mine, the failure is not mine, but the two together make me.'

Estella says this to Miss Havisham after Miss Havisham complains that Estella treats her coldly and without love. Estella is astonished that her adopted mother would make such an accusation after deliberately raising her to avoid emotional attachment. Miss Havisham, Estella realises, has encouraged her to treat those who love her with deliberate cruelty. Estella tells Miss Havisham that she has made her as she is. Estella is both Miss Havisham's success and her failure. The quotation shows that Estella has gradually realised who she is, and this will help her to grow into a better person.

4 'Look'ee here, Pip. I'm your second father. You're my son — more to me nor any son. I've put away money, only for you to spend. When I was a hired-out shepherd in a solitary hut, not seeing no faces but faces of sheep till I half-forgot wot men's and women's faces wos like, I see yourn ... I see you there a many times plain as ever I see you on them misty marshes. 'Lord strike me dead!' I says each time — and I goes out in the open air to say it under the open heavens — 'but wot, if I gets liberty and money, I'll make that boy a gentleman!'

Magwitch makes this speech to Pip when he reveals himself as Pip's secret supporter. Magwitch is the reason why Pip is wealthy. This is important, because it means Pip must lose his idealistic visions. He is forced to realise he is only a gentleman because of a criminal.

5 'Dear Magwitch, I must tell you, now at last. You understand what I say?'
A gentle pressure on my hand.
'You had a child once, whom you loved and lost.'
A stronger pressure on my hand.
'She lived and found powerful friends. She is living now. She is a lady and very beautiful. And I love her!'

In this quotation, Pip tells the dying Magwitch about his daughter, Estella, whom he has not seen since she was very young. By reassuring the dying Magwitch with the truth about Estella, Pip shows how much he has matured. He has a new understanding of what matters in life. Rather than insisting on the social class that has guided him throughout life, Pip now values loyalty, love and inner goodness.

Notes

Audio Track Listings

Great Expectations

CD 1

Track 1 Copyright info
Track 1 Volume I Chapter I
Track 2 Volume I Chapter II
Track 3 Volume I Chapter III
Track 4 Volume I Chapter IV
Track 5 Volume I Chapter V
Track 6 Volume I Chapter VI
Track 7 Volume I Chapter VII
Track 8 Volume I Chapter VIII
Track 9 Volume I Chapter IX
Track 10 Volume I Chapter X
Track 11 Volume I Chapter XI
Track 12 Volume I Chapter XII
Track 13 Volume I Chapter XIII
Track 14 Volume I Chapter XIV
Track 15 Volume I Chapter XV
Track 16 Volume I Chapter XVI
Track 17 Volume I Chapter XVII
Track 18 Volume I Chapter XVIII
Track 19 Volume I Chapter XIX

CD 2

Track 1 Volume II Chapter I
Track 2 Volume II Chapter II
Track 3 Volume II Chapter III
Track 4 Volume II Chapter IV
Track 5 Volume II Chapter V
Track 6 Volume II Chapter VI
Track 7 Volume II Chapter VII
Track 8 Volume II Chapter VIII
Track 9 Volume II Chapter IX
Track 10 Volume II Chapter X
Track 11 Volume II Chapter XI
Track 12 Volume II Chapter XII
Track 13 Volume II Chapter XIII
Track 14 Volume II Chapter XIV
Track 15 Volume II Chapter XV
Track 16 Volume II Chapter XVI
Track 17 Volume II Chapter XVII
Track 18 Volume II Chapter XVIII
Track 19 Volume II Chapter XIX
Track 20 Volume II Chapter XX

CD 3

Track 1 Volume III Chapter I
Track 2 Volume III Chapter II
Track 3 Volume III Chapter III
Track 4 Volume III Chapter IV
Track 5 Volume III Chapter V
Track 6 Volume III Chapter VI
Track 7 Volume III Chapter VII
Track 8 Volume III Chapter VIII
Track 9 Volume III Chapter IX
Track 10 Volume III Chapter X
Track 11 Volume III Chapter XI
Track 12 Volume III Chapter XII
Track 13 Volume III Chapter XIII
Track 14 Volume III Chapter XIV
Track 15 Volume III Chapter XV
Track 16 Volume III Chapter XVI
Track 17 Volume III Chapter XVII
Track 18 Volume III Chapter XVIII
Track 19 Volume III Chapter XIX
Track 20 Volume III Chapter XX

OTHER CLASSICAL COMICS TITLES:

Henry V

Available now

Macbeth

Available now

Frankenstein

Available now